OBJECTIVITY, EMPIRICISM AND TRUTH

STUDIES IN
PHILOSOPHICAL PSYCHOLOGY

Edited by

R. F. HOLLAND

OBJECTIVITY, EMPIRICISM AND TRUTH

by

R. W. NEWELL

ROUTLEDGE & KEGAN PAUL
LONDON AND NEW YORK

First published in 1986 by
Routledge & Kegan Paul plc
11 New Fetter Lane, London EC4P 4EE
Published in the USA by
Routledge & Kegan Paul Inc.
in association with Methuen Inc.
29 West 35th Street, New York, NY 10001

Set in 10 on 12 pt Monophoto Baskerville
and printed and bound in Great Britain
by Butler & Tanner Ltd,
Frome, and London

Library of Congress Cataloging in Publication Data

Newell, R. W.
Objectivity, empiricism, and truth.

(Studies in philosophical psychology)
Bibliography: p.
Includes index.
1. Objectivity—Addresses, essays, lectures.   2. Certainty—
Addresses, essays, lectures.   3. Reasoning—Addresses, essays,
lectures.   4. Relativity—Addresses, essays, lectures.
I. Title.   II. Series.
BD220.N48 1986   121   85-28182

British Library CIP Data also available
ISBN 0-7102-0897-9

CONTENTS

ACKNOWLEDGMENTS

I am grateful to Renford Bambrough for his encouragement and good advice, and to Roy Holland for his invaluable suggestions and his editorial patience. An earlier version of part of Chapter 5 was presented to a conference on John Wisdom at Trinity College. Cambridge, and subsequently published under the title 'The Scope of Reason' in *Philosophy of Life, Essays on John Wisdom*, ed. I. Dilman, Nijhoff, 1984.

INTRODUCTION

The need to find new bearings in the topics of objectivity, certainty, reasoning and relativism is the excuse for the discussions to follow. We need not look for new faces. Wittgenstein, William James, John Wisdom and Thomas Kuhn are the heroes of this book for a reason of particular importance. They share an attitude towards epistemological problems which is fundamentally in conflict with the empiricist tradition, and in the conflict a fresh message emerges. The concepts central to epistemology – knowledge, truth, certainty, objectivity – cannot be appreciated for what they are without understanding their connections with human actions. The work of these philosophers is marked by a shift away from the foundationalist vision of empirical knowledge funded by perceptual data. It is part of a movement towards a broadly conceived idea that people and their practices matter as much, if not more, than the justification of beliefs. If they are right, there is no returning to the classical route from sensations to knowledge by way of tiers of justifiable inference; the road brilliantly pioneered by the old empiricists leads to the wrong set of answers.

The fabric of a philosopher's work is not, or hardly ever is, a seamless piece without changes of weave, improvements and second thoughts. In this book Wittgenstein is the Wittgenstein of *On Certainty*, and James is the James of *Pragmatism;* Wisdom is viewed through his later writing and the glimpses of Kuhn are equally selective. Chapter 1, 'The human contribution', is an introduction to the leading idea, found in James and Kuhn, that an epistemology valuing an impersonal control over beliefs is one best set aside. The second chapter links objectivity with action. It argues that objectivity is a practice of people and not a self-transcending property, and that the objectiveness of a person lies in a preparedness to respect the constraints of reason impartially. Chapter 3 glances at Quine and the prospects for an enlightened pragmatism. Observation attaches our claims to the world but does not make them true, and we can stay with James and Quine in affirming that pragmatic adjustments across our fields of belief, together with certain virtues of method, will suffice for the extraction of any truths essential to organizing experience to the best advantage. But we can stay with them only up to a point, since pragmatism can avoid a permissive conception of truth only by acknowledging that some things are unassailably certain, and here James and Quine balk. Wittgenstein's solution to the problem of certainty is the topic of the fourth chapter. He sketches a conception of certainty deriving from a pragmatic explanation of people's actions, one independent of procedures of evidence and justification whose very possibility, he argues, presupposes a primary place for human action in epistemology.

Chapter 5 shows how the constraints of reason that objectiveness imposes on us ultimately resolve into a respect for the constraints of particular cases, as Wisdom has argued. Because there can be no discussions among people unless practices of the kind to which Wisdom points are respected, the last chapter agrees both with relativism's claim that ways of reasoning vary with the styles of the reasoners, and with rationalism's claim that all reasoners must share some common ground. And if Wittgenstein is right, the context-dependency of reasons does not prevent rational discussions across radically different cultures or points of view.

CHAPTER 1

THE HUMAN CONTRIBUTION:
WILLIAM JAMES AND THOMAS KUHN

After every circumstance, every relation is known, the understanding has no room to operate, nor any object on which it could employ itself. Hume, *Enquiry Concerning the Principles of Morals*, Appendix I.

You can't weed out the human contribution. William James, *Pragmatism*.

It is an odd twist of circumstance that Hume, who gave so much importance to the psychology of individual agents in the determination of belief, should have prepared the way for a sophisticated attitude in philosophy deserving of James' rebuke. It is at least generally thought to have been Hume's intention to reveal how it is that beliefs closed to confirmation by observation or logical demonstration must be beyond the scope of reason, their assertion being at best an expression of subjective attitude or feeling. And this limitation has had the effect, which to Hume's mind would have been a curious one, of bringing about a picture of philosophy increasingly requiring the elimination of the 'human contribution' so important to James. Even if we deplore this 'Humean' picture as just so much flawed verificationism we cannot casually dismiss it, for there is a deep sense in which philosophy has yet to adapt to, and feel at ease with, a conception of rational argument free from the weight of Hume's constraints. Despite the exorcism of positivism from philosophy there is still much plausibility in the thought that, although wrong in many of its details, the general lines of the Humean recipe are sound. We need controls on argument if evidence, justification and proof are to be within reach, and what Hume seems to offer is a cogent defence against an anarchy in which anything goes.

So the recipe still grips firmly, and one sign of its life is the philosophical reception given to certain views of Thomas Kuhn. He is seen to have transgressed the dogma that what is outside logic and observation is outside rationality, and the *locus* of the offence is his account of theory-choice. Kuhn's strategy, say his critics, makes choices between theories personal, psychological or subjective; they cannot be based on good reasons, there can be no objective control by shared observation or common standards; there is 'no room for any sort of rational deliberation' and decisions in science must, if Kuhn is right, be regarded as arbitrary in the end, and 'are in no better state than those of religion'.[1]

Strong stuff, but surprisingly it seems to be vindicated by premises which Kuhn himself supplies. For he insists that 'the issue of paradigm choice can never be unequivocally settled by logic and experiment alone' and 'debates over theory choice cannot be cast in a form that fully resembles logical or mathematical proof'. With deductive prooof and observation curbed there is 'an absence of criteria able to dictate the choice of each individual'; and when he claims that in place of appeal to logic and experience we have recourse to persuasion, it is excusable that Humean intuitions should unite in the thought that Kuhn has altogether priced himself outside reason's range.

Kuhn's own defence is disarming. There are indeed more or less standard and rational criteria for evaluating theories – accuracy, consistency, simplicity, scope, fruitfulness and perhaps others. And this is safe enough. But then all seems undermined when he tells us that they function as value judgments influencing choices, like heuristic maxims guiding but not dictating decisions. These criteria are open to varying and individual interpretation; they rely, in part, 'on idiosyn-

cratic factors dependent upon individual biography and personality'. Kuhn's urbane assurance that nothing in this thesis
implies that good and decisive reasons are no longer to be
found has seemed astonishing to his critics. And with the door
to subjectivism apparently wide open, astonishment is understandable.[2]

Kuhn's recent adventures were foreshadowed around the
turn of the century by William James's protracted struggle to
convince *his* critics of the soundness of much the same point,
namely that a commitment to what seems like 'subjectivism'
is not a commitment to abandoning rationality. W. K. Clifford
– in a sense James's Hume – affirmed that it is always wrong
to believe anything on insufficient evidence – evidence less
than that of experience or valid argument. James's rejection of
this claim is sharp and puzzling. On the contrary, he tells us,
it can be right to believe things on other than the 'intellectual
grounds' praised by Clifford.[3] With the glove thus thrown down,
the pressing question for James is *when* is it right, and why?

When a proposition, whose resolution has consequences of
importance, is not capable of being decided by experience or
logic it is right, James thinks, that it should be decided by 'our
passional nature'. Otherwise we run the risk of missing a truth
that matters. Appeal to the passions, or to what James was
later to call 'satisfaction', he saw as a legitimate and rational
mode of justification. Of course, the thesis needs the developed
support which it subsequently gets in *Pragmatism* where James's
theory of evidence undergoes a major change. The earlier
view that psychologically determined judgments stand outside
science and logic, which looks back towards Peirce, is aban-
doned in favour of a thorough-going holism in which the sentiments become evidence on a par with all other evidence. A
person may find a belief psychologically satisfactory because
it enables him to organize his view of the world in a way that
makes sense to him by making 'advantageous connections' between the various parts of it. And it does seem right to say
that the practical consequences of a belief in facilitating an

understanding of experience are no less 'psychological' than any consequences it may have for the emotions; the sentiments may rule the head and not just the heart in making adjustments between background and current experience. In a striking anticipation of the holistic elements in Quine's epistemology James argues that the test of true belief is a matter of accommodating fresh observations within a body of existing opinion and in this 'consistency between previous truth and novel fact is always the most imperious claimant'. Although assimilation may require the revision of old beliefs to preserve new experiences, the converse too may hold; as with Quine, observation and theory may each tug the other and the limits of adjustment are tempered by conservatism.[4]

The resemblance to Quine abruptly ceases with James's rejection of behaviourism in favour of a central role for, as he calls them, 'subjective' reasons in the verification process. And here, as with Kuhn, is where the trouble starts. For James says 'sometimes alternative theoretic formulas are equally compatible with all the truths we know and then we choose between them for subjective reasons'.[5] These reasons turn out to coincide roughly with the standard list which Kuhn gives for theory evaluation and by using them 'we choose the kind of theory to which we are already partial'. As James sees it, reasons like these remain 'subjective' in the sense that their success or failure is a 'a matter for individual appreciation'. Like Kuhn he insists that they are reasons as much as any other reasons. Once again the astonishment of the critics is understandable.

At issue in all of this is a controversy reflecting a deeply-seated division in philosophical attitudes with fundamental issues at stake. There is a strong temptation to suppose that behind pragmatist and Kuhnian structures are assumptions essentially like those of traditional empiricism. This misconception partly accounts for the irritation often infusing criticism and is largely a consequence of the history of the opposing views. The critics enter the debate armed with an epistemological tradition surviving a century of discussion, one by now second nature. The views of Kuhn and James are buttressed by less rich resources. To be sure, there is a wealth of empiricist theory on which to build, but it is the wrong theory even if it is the most comprehensive one at hand. In *The Structure of Scientific Revolutions* Kuhn suffered from the lack of an articulated epistemology and the omission, excusable enough, was costly; for the missing background was naturally filled-in by contemporary theorizing of a kind that could lead only to disaffection. It is significant that in quarters outside philosophy where there is no particular commitment to foundationalist ideas Kuhn's reception was enthusiastic.

There is a special reason for paying attention to James. Contemporary interest in pragmatism is largely Peircean-centred or focused on a generalized thesis summed-up recently in Rorty's slogan that there are 'no constraints on inquiry save conversational ones'.[6] Peirce's vision of inquiry is fundamentally at odds with James's and is too close to orthodox outlooks to guide an epistemology breaking away from tradition. To come to grips with James by backward references to Peirce in his early papers is to forget Peirce's own exasperation with the wayward direction he saw James take, and James's waywardness marks a departure from the premises which make Peirce's view so approachable to neo-positivist thinking. Rorty is more faithful to James's instincts but his distillation of the pragmatist core owes less to *Pragmatism* than to a larger un-Jamesian picture of philosophy. There is no easy model to help us grasp James's view, save in the case of Quine; and it is not surprising that the elements in Quine's philosophy which effectively light up James's rambling presentation should be the ones most in conflict with modern foundationalism.

James's importance lies in his determined attempt to shape epistemology around human actions and practices without sacrificing rational control over the acceptance or rejection of beliefs. The problems which bothered him endlessly centred on the issues of rationalism, idealism and empiricism as they were perceived by his contemporaries at the turn of the century.

Pragmatism was at the time an *avant-garde* philosophy knock-
ing hard, largely through James's efforts, at the door of the
establishment with a message that gave no comfort to the
established views. It is not surprising that it should have been
officially resisted and usually misunderstood, or that *Pragmatism* should be generously provisioned with James's characteristic brand of polemical persuasion. It is probably true that
Pragmatism can be read with justice to James only with the
advantage of hindsight separating the domestic issues embroil-
ing him with his contemporaries from a view of permanent
importance. His lectures on *Pragmatism* were given in Boston
in 1906 and again in New York in 1907, and they had a
curiously ironic fate still influencing their reception. It was
James's hope to make philosophy accessible to a general public
audience hence the need, as he saw it, for popular and
approachable lectures affirming American philosophical conceptions to mainly lay audiences ill-disposed to academic
speculation. 'Some of my colleagues may possibly shake their
heads at this', he writes, 'but on taking my cue from what has
seemed to me to be the feeling of the audiences, I believe that
I am shaping my books so as to satisfy the general public
need.'[7] If philosophy has value it should survive a removal
from the ivory tower, James thought, and what its popular
exposition may lose in terms of the 'refinement' of European-
based idealism and rationalism, which his public audiences
distained, will be more than made up by a robust respect for
reality and by the expression of points in popular idiom. 'A
philosophy that breathes nothing but refinement', he says, 'will
seem a monument of artificiality. So we find men of science
preferring to turn their backs on metaphysics as on something
altogether cloistered and spectral, and practical men shaking
philosophy's dust off their feet and following the call of the
wild.'[8] It would be a disaster if practical men rejected philosophy altogether and James viewed his evangelical public lec-
turing as one way of preventing it. But the scheme backfired
badly. The academics despaired at the spectacle of a great

psychologist gone astray and condemned the lectures. The lay public acclaimed them with enthusiasm but took away only what they wanted to hear, which had little to do with the message. James complained bitterly, 'The pragmatism that lies inside *me* is so different from that of which I succeed in wakening the idea inside other people, that this makes me feel like cursing God and dying.'[9]

Divisions in attitude are deeper than differences in theory and more diffuse. Because of this they risk going unsaid. The distance separating James and Kuhn from their critics reflects, with some bending of doctrine, a split between pragmatism and foundationalism. The characterization is rough, as needs be, and is of less importance than an underlying difference which really does matter. In its general aspect orthodox empiricism accounts for knowledge of the world through a layer-like structure of linear inference terminating in a base of sense-experience. Observers apprehend, sense, become acquainted with or directly intuit a 'presentational continuum' of given perceptual data, sense-contents or representations constituting their immediate experience. The leading metaphor is that of the reception of sensory data by an individual agent; how far the eye of the mind aids the eye itself was always an issue, but one largely unaffecting the picture of a sensory, or sensory-cum-intellectual confrontation with the world as it is perceived. At the base of inference to knowledge, perceiving persons monitor and report their experiences.

There is another way of looking at knowledge because there is another way of looking at persons. We may see them as agents acting in the world and guided by their beliefs, motives, desires and needs; and thus seen, explain epistemological ideas by focusing on human activities and practices. Reasoning, observing, judging and the quality of 'being objective' are products of people's activities and we can, as Wittgenstein argued, look to our acting and not to a kind of seeing in explaining certainty. He tapped a rich and underexplored vein by realigning the question 'What makes rational justification possible?'

as the question 'What sort of human practices make it possible?' The epistemological perspective shifts away from the
image of the subjective observer facing an objective outside
world and towards a conception of consciously active agents
acting rationally against a background of acquired belief.

Both these attitudes value the virtues of objectivity, reasoning and the assignment of truth-values by rational methods.
The problem for the latter – the 'humanistic' attitude, as
James sometimes called it – is the difficulty of placing people
at the focus of epistemology without rejecting these virtues or
placing them seriously at risk. It is not surprising that the
attempt should seem misconceived in the light of the orthodox
view that subject-related elements accruing from James's
'human contribution' undercut interpersonally neutral testing
and permit the observer to project his own beliefs onto the
world: it seems to dodge the issue of rational control over the
conclusions people may reach. The accusation is important.
James separated philosophers into people with two sorts of
temperament; tough and tender minded, vividly collecting the
mental make-up of rival approaches in a memorable image.
He says, 'The one thing that has *counted* so far in philosophy
is that a man should *see* things, see them straight in his own
peculiar way, and be dissatisfied with any opposite way of
seeing them.'[10] The issue of 'rational control' is divided by just
such different ways of seeing and defines the distance between
the 'humanists' on the one hand, and their critics on the other.
At stake is a matter of discipline viewed in two ways. We can,
with the critics, seek rational control by the *independent* discipline of rules, standards, general criteria or premises and
favour deductive algorithms or unrevisable observational control as a way of securing it. Alternatively we can with the
humanists look for *self*-discipline as a control over the rationality of beliefs and favour discussion, argument, decision and
judgment constrained by consistency and the limits of intelligible adjustment.

The unlabelled opposition to foundationalist empiricism is

an epistemological coalition with James, Kuhn, Wittgenstein and Wisdom as the front benchers, and the choice of just these four records their own distinctive and original moves to a discernibly joint end. They have no common programmatic doctrine beyond the message that an epistemology from which the human element is persistently 'weeded out' is a sad confidence trick. James's warning against weeding out the human contribution in philosophy is a fundamental criticism of the price to be paid for a developed empiricism. It opposes the thought that a subject matter open to uniform testing can be achieved only if the road to objectivity coincides with the road to impersonality, and that true and objective beliefs can be secured by progressively eliminating subject-related factors from the process of verification, those personal factors of background, biography, values, attitude, ability, decision and judgment which are distinctive of 'oneself'. It was James's profound hope to put people back into epistemology, hence the centrality of his conflict with theories, which, if they are to survive as cogent accounts of what it is to test something, require that people should be eased out of the way.

Broadly speaking, this requirement is implemented in terms of two strategic moves, the shift to generality and the shift to pure perception. Objective control over judgments is sought in universal criteria and neutral observation; one looks up to premises or rules to control identification and inference, and looks down to a base of sensory data to control truth-values. Both act as common measures for testing which will be free from personal idiosyncrasy. The generality shift represents the essentialist element which James tirelessly fought. The motive for his opposition was not simply that he thought essentialism to be false, but came from what he saw to be a more insidious danger. One may indeed appeal to premises, rules and general criteria of identification, but one cannot ultimately do so. Appeal to principles to validate decisions takes over the role of individual responsibility for judgment. The burden of decision is shifted from ascribing agents to prescriptive rules and ascribers become operators of a decision-making apparatus in which responsibility is taken out of their hands. James thought that the restoration of human responsibility is essential for epistemological success. Empiricist strategy generates a dichotomy of the analytic-synthetic type in which each direction of discourse has its own mode of validation. When James boasted that his theory was 'democratic' he was opposing any such dichotomy in the interests of a uniform account of testing, and the rejection of the analytic-synthetic distinction is one identifying mark of pragmatism in all its forms. Yet the core of James' opposition, of which the scrapping of this distinction is a consequence, remains in his repudiation of the thought that the key to epistemological success lies in increasingly impersonalized judgment.

Like James, Kuhn insists that an account of science is unacceptable if the personal elements of values and background are excluded from it. Both logic and psychology direct choices, he thinks, and the thesis is expanded into a confrontation with essentialist attitudes. The question of how scientists can identify and agree upon terms appropriate to fresh problems is not to be answered by reference to defining conditions but ultimately by appealing to similarities and differences between cases. In his article 'Second Thoughts on Paradigms' Kuhn argues that a scientist or a student confronted with a problem 'seeks to see it as like one or more of the exemplary problems he has encountered before'. This is unexceptional enough, but how is the scientist or the student able to do this? Kuhn rejects the traditional answer: 'I attack the often implicit assumption that anyone who knows how to use a basic term correctly has access, conscious or unconscious, to a set of criteria which define that term or provide necessary and sufficient conditions governing its application.' The view is worth quoting fully: 'His (the student's) basic criterion is a perception of similarity that is both logically and psychologically prior to any of the numerous criteria by which that same identification of similarity might have been made. After the similarity has been seen, one may ask for criteria and it is then often worth doing so. But one need not.' And he adds, 'there is a means of processing data into similarity sets which does not depend on a prior answer to the question, similar with respect to what?' What *is* fundamental, Kuhn maintains, is the assimilation of examples shared by a community of ascribers relying on the acquired perception of comparable cases; 'I continue to insist that shared examples have essential cognitive functions prior to a specification of criteria with respect to which they are exemplary.'[11]

The orthodox defence of objectivity relies on two ideas, the maintenance of interpersonal commensurability – of perceptions, meanings and beliefs – and the elimination of whatever might break down this commensurability. One way of achieving commensurability is to hold that general criteria of identification shared across the board are necessary for the justified ascription of predicates; the verdicts of different individuals thus become measurable by the same standard. And one way of avoiding a breakdown is to eliminate divisive subjective elements from the decision-making process. In short, the slogan is up with unity and down with fragmentation. Kuhn's arguments strike directly at this scheme, but not in a way that replaces the slogan by its anarchistic converse. He was shrewd enough to see that once tied to the sharing of generalizations, standards and rules, commensurability becomes unattainable and the very safeguards against fragmentation introduced to put commensurability on a secure footing actually ensure that it is beyond reach. We can do better to see it as a shared respect for differences and a common preparedness to discuss them from divergent perspectives. Like John Wisdom he argues that reliance on the recognition of parallels and differences should displace appeal to criteria on key occasions of perceptual identification. Words must attach to the world and there remains, as Kuhn says, a 'minimum stable element' to which predicates stick as firmly as predicates can; for we may take, as basic language units, references to those units of experience which are seen as being identifying exemplars without the aid of generalizations.

In Wisdom's hands the idea grows into a bold re-evaluation of the epistemological role of deductive inference. He claims that logically valid forms of inference occur inessentially with respect to the certainty of an argument. There is no going back to the idea that logical validity exemplifies reason's strongest constraint on our ascriptive decisions and this point is central to the larger issue of divergence in attitude between a humanistic approach and that of traditional foundationalism. It is central because the obvious objection to the incipient 'looseness' of a Kuhn-Wisdom prescription can be put in a broadly generalized way by saying that we are left with no objective control over the conclusions people may reach. Properly translated, the objection makes the point that final control over our decisions cannot rest with our premises since our premises are themselves subject to our self-disciplined opinions about their value. The question for Wisdom and Kuhn, and for pragmatists generally, is what this self-discipline must be like.

Yet the issue of *truth* remains a hurdle and Kuhn is oddly silent save for a casual rejection of correspondence theories. For James the issue of truth is a topic of extensive discussion. It is central to his thesis, troublesome and embodies the main doctrinal divide between him and his opponents. It is also an issue surviving unresolved despite James's optimism. Truth, he says, is 'a matter of gratifying the individual's desire to assimilate the novel in his experience' and this gives a clue to the trouble to follow. Characteristically the 'human element' is built into the notion of truth and truth-testing; empiricism's rejection of subjectivity is a discredited option, so James is left with the choice, which pragmatists of any stripe must face, of deciding where truth-control really lies, in personal belief or impersonal reality. James's unpromising answer goes between the alternatives. Both beliefs and reality are inseparable from the contributions of individuals; 'the trail of the human serpent is thus over everything' and the obvious question is whether this prescription can leave judgments in contact with the world at all. A major attraction of correspondence theories is simply that this question is a much less obvious one to ask, for the evidence of testing is independent of the beliefs to be tested. At least that is the intention, and James was among the first to spot its flaws in a discussion of 'theory-ladenness' which more recent work has not improved. But this pushes him deeper into the difficulty of cogently accounting for truth without fatal circularity. The correspondence relation is 'static', he thinks, whereas truth-testing properly embodies a plastic relation between background beliefs and current experiences with each subject to alteration by the action of the other. There are constraints, notably a conservatism in favour of adjustments between new observation and received beliefs which would 'derange common sense and previous beliefs as little as possible'. The aim is to promote intelligibility, and to preserve the consistency upon which intelligibility rests, for an incoherent set of beliefs about the world produces an incoherent world to the believer, one unsatisfying and going against native desires. False beliefs fail to gratify because they fail to be useful in structuring one's picture of the world in a way that makes sense. Here James's consequentialism comes into play, since the main requirement of an intelligible world is the ability to anticipate and predict events. A breakdown in this signals unsatisfying disorder and ultimately a total inability to cope; the remedy is to readjust the interlock of beliefs and observations to restore predictability, and this may occasion the filtering out of ill-fitting beliefs. Hence truth is useful; and the idea of the 'utility of truth' is little more than the reflection that the capacity of a belief system to say what is coming next, and why, is an excellent measure of its truth-content.

This reflection may recall Peirce's operationalist programme in the papers which James knew about.[12] The comparison is misleading, for a reading of James shows throughout that the criteria of control are for him psychological, a most un-

Peircean thought exposed in their different approaches to consequentialism. When Peirce prescribed that in testing we must heed the logical consequences of the propositions we believe, James replied that we must heed the psychological consequences of believing the propositions we do. The emphasis and the doctrine are wide apart. And, to borrow a phrase from James, it is just this difference which makes the difference. The importance of predictiveness lies in its consequences *for us* as agents possessing values, beliefs, desires and attitudes. And these will, naturally, vary with individuals and their backgrounds, abilities and expectations; the uniformity of the consequences of beliefs will be no greater than the uniformity of the believers themselves. For this reason a test of true belief cannot be a straightforward process of conjecture and refutation, or confirmation, by experience; experiences depend on the experiencers and the results of such testing remain open to individual interpretation.

James was troubled by the understandable criticism that pragmatists lose touch with reality, so much so that his efforts to stress that factual beliefs require 'direct face-to-face verification somewhere' verge on the heroic. 'Truth lives', he says, 'for the most part on a credit system.' Beliefs are like bank cheques whose credibility turns on a guarantee of payment; they pass because they can be cashed eventually by eye-witness encounters on demand. The metaphor might apply aptly to any theory pushing a verifiability requirement for empirical statements, including the empiricism he opposes. So where does the conflict lie? James was determined to hold on to the 'human contribution' in verification at any cost. An easy way out at this stage of his scheme would have been possible, for he might have sacrificed the individualism so well protected up to now by cutting it back in 'face-to-face' sensory confrontations. To do this would be to throw in the towel, as James knew, and transform his pragmatism into a curiously articulated version of the empiricism he was set against. It is standard fare in empiricist theorizing to graft a coherence structure

onto a sense-datum base. But this, James thinks, would preserve all the old evils. It would in addition falsify much of what
we know about perception. Pragmatically speaking, we have
the option of choosing a sense-datum type answer given the
repudiation of other facts inconsistent with it; we choose the
theory that gives the best accommodation to our stock of beliefs
both past and incoming. But the pull of these other facts is too
strong and their sacrifice too disruptive: 'Although the stub-
born fact remains that there *is* a sensible flux, what is *true of it*
seems from first to last to be largely a matter of our own
creation.' It is an inescapable fact that perception is infused
with our beliefs and to affirm this, as James does, is to eliminate the option of ascribing truth at the point of contact with
the given. Yet this triumph over the sense-datum base idea is
double edged. It renews the force of the criticism that James
has prised us off the world; a philosopher who insists that 'We
create the subjects of our true as well as of our false propositions'
has arguably relinquished all objective control over belief.[13]

The 'humanistic' account threatens philosophical values by
making it seem hard, if not impossible, to stay with the conviction that some things *are* true, and are true for all men
whether they realize it or not. James and Wittgenstein appreciated that to understand this conviction one must first understand why it is held; that the question 'Why should a person
become convinced of such a thing?' is as important as the
question 'Is it correct or not?', and that the two questions are
much more closely linked than orthodox empiricism would
allow. The linkage is traditionally suspect because the latter
question is one about reasons for beliefs whereas the former
asks why people stick with beliefs, and the answers may be
different in each case. But there is nothing to prevent one
arguing, as Wittgenstein does, that reasons for a belief termi-
nate in the actions and practices of the believers, thus tying
the questions together with the Jamesian thought that there is
no reasoning without reasoners and that 'reasoners' are people
acting under the constraints of their current stock of opinions.

CHAPTER 2

THE TWO FACES OF OBJECTIVITY

The idea of objectivity is handed down to us bearing two generically different faces. One of them is a source of self-imposed puzzlement and guides directly to foundationalism. Objectivity's other face is altogether different; it is central to our concerns and indispensable to our actions as rational beings.

The first face of objectivity is an essentially technical conception attached to philosophy most influentially since Kant. It gives objectivity two roles. First, an ontological role ascribing objectivity to 'objects', or particular bodies, entities, complexes or states of affairs existing apart from perceptions more or less continuously in space and time, falling under the heading of 'objective particulars'. And second, an epistemological role in which objectivity is ascribed to items of a different sort, beliefs, judgments, propositions or products of thought about what is really the case, forming a general class of 'objective judgments'. The two roles become linked when objective particulars are seen as the topics of objective judgments and, thus linked, 'objectivity' becomes an explanatory notion.

The positing of an objective world of particulars independent of experience is intended to account for experience as we have it. Objective particulars seem required if there is to be any explanation of how different impressions taken to be representations of the world are to have a unity ensuring identity through change, or any explanation of beliefs about the continuous and independent existence of real objects. And they seem needed if cogency is to be given to the idea that judgments about the real world can be independent of judgments about particular states of awareness or experience. For this could not occur, it seems, unless an aggregative structure of outer things and their properties provide a stable referential framework for the ascription of predicates, as well as the means by which assertions of fact can have truth-values irrespective of the beliefs of individuals. Objective particulars are needed as the correlates of objective judgments to explain how experiences can suceed or fail to represent the world.

Central to this picture of objectivity is the requirement that beliefs about an objective world must hold good independently of the experiences, or particular states of mind, on which people may rely for their assertion. This fastening of objectivity to impersonality is a common premise of different epistemologies. Although Locke took personal experiences to differ in the extent to which they are trustworthy indicators of an impersonal external world, he nevertheless honoured the premise in his account of representation. And Kant held that even if experience has to possess the connectedness of a unified world, judgments about objects, if they are objective, hold independently of the occurrence of any experiences of them. The intention is to dissociate objective judgments from any essential connection with the opinions and experiences of persons, or from anything that can be called 'oneself'.

Objectivity's second face is a largely untechnical conception, on the whole thought to be of less philosophical interest than the first one. Objective judgments are contrasted with prejudiced, biased or dogmatic judgments and objectivity is associated with impartiality, detachment, disinterestedness and a willingness to submit to standards of evidence. It is distinctive of this view that objectivity attaches to *persons* through their actions. What makes a judgment objective is not something special about outer objects, but something special about people's practices. Seen in this way objectivity is an inter-personal notion, giving sense to the idea that a person may be, or may become objective by the exercise of a disposition to act within the constraints of a wider social practice. Just as, for example, honesty is associated with identifiable patterns of behaviour within a network of practice so, in this view, objectiveness is identified by a respect for certain norms, and among them are standards of evidence and argument regulating ways of resolving disputes, settling issues and deciding beliefs. A person may be encouraged or taught to be objective; he may learn to be, for example, by trying to free himself from the bias of his beliefs; he may choose to be objective, much as he may choose to be honest; and he can be commended for his objectivity, for we see objectivity as being a desirable quality in a person. In these cases the earlier ontological role is displaced by a normative one attaching objectivity to people and their actions. 'Objectivity' becomes a quality of character applied or withheld on the evidence of what one does.

Thus the two 'faces' face the world differently. On the first view, objectivity will depend upon the existence of impersonal entities and is independent of subject-related properties; on the second view it is dependent upon the performance of human actions and bound up with choices and decisions. The temptation to think of these two faces in terms of alternative senses of the word 'objective' should be resisted. Much more is at stake. We are presented with rival conceptions of objectivity organizing and shaping a central range of epistemological issues, compelling 'pictures', in Wittgenstein's phrase, carrying different philosophical commitments.

Which picture should influence the attitude and direction of our thinking about objectivity? Pragmatism prescribes that objectivity must have a useful place in our thinking if it is to have any place in our thinking. It must not be, in Wittgenstein's sense, 'idle' and the idea of objectiveness should pay its way. The trouble with the first, technical, version is just that it fails to do this. It invokes objectivity as an explanation of the coherence, uniformity and identity of perceptions and of the difference between what is appearance and what is not;

objectivity characterizes 'what is really out there' thus separating it from what is locked in awareness. Yet the explanatory burden is carried by the idea of external existence alone with 'objectivity' tagging along gratuitously. What is actually offered as an explanation of experience is a posited domain of enduring outer objects and properties, a reality independent of experience which descriptions relying on perceptions may fit or fail to fit. In this there is no distinctive job for the notion of objectivity beyond the job already performed by the notion of independent particulars; the question 'What is it for something to be objective?' becomes the question 'What is it for something to be external, independent of consciousness or really out there?' The problem of accounting for the objectivity of particulars emerges as just being the problem of accounting for the externality and independence of particulars; and the reciprocal connection fastens them together in such a way that the latter problem cannot be elucidated informatively by terms referring to objectivity without the resulting circularity. On the one hand it is held that what makes a particular an objective one is its enduring, mind-independent status and, on the other hand, that this special status is explained by a particular's possession of objective properties. The two 'explanations' trade on each other, and the interdefinability of these notions prevents the idea of objectivity from fulfilling an independent role.

To explain 'things as they really are' by calling them 'objective' accomplishes nothing without a prior grasp of the difference between 'real things' and representations, and if we already have a sense of that distinction then there is no need to invoke the notion of objectivity to provide it. Nor does it help to define a subjective-objective difference by an inner-outer contrast. Defined in this way, the question 'What is the difference between the subjective and the objective?' is answered comprehensively by answering the counterpart question 'What is the difference between the inner and the outer?' Every problem or query about the one is a problem or query about the other, and nothing of an explanatory nature is gained by the translation. Objectivity's first face makes objectivity a redundant concept. It is replaceable by the notions it tries to explain, and to characterize 'the problem of the external world' as 'the problem of objectivity' is just to redescribe the issue.

That the notions of objectivity and externality are often taken to be roughly interchangeable is not surprising, yet this very interchangeability must leave objectivity without a distinctive job of its own. It might be allowed that the term 'objectivity', as it is used in the context of the first picture, has a broadly summarizing function and serves as a kind of shorthand description of what would otherwise be a more prolix statement. One may grant it the status of a *façon de parler* and speak of 'objective particulars' or of 'objectivity concepts' when what is meant are particulars or concepts retaining their existence or validity independently of human experiences or beliefs. That the term does have this summarizing role to a large extent in philosophical writing emphasizes again its essential redundancy, for it could possess such a role only if it is implicitly recognized as a near-replacement for the more lengthy stories it abbreviates. The first of objectivity's two faces is of little interest beyond any interest there may be in the issues of outer objects and their representation.

Nevertheless it may continue to influence attempts to preserve the independence of beliefs from things outside them by broadly identifying objective particulars with 'the facts'. For it may be thought that the objectivity of an empirical judgment is ensured if it successfully mirrors the facts which it is about, giving it a topic of reference independent of awareness. The search for objectivity would, once again, be a search for 'real' properties guaranteeing interpersonal commensurability.

The importance of facts is usually seen to lie in the capacity to explain truth. Since the evidence for the truth of a judgment about the world lies elsewhere than in its being asserted or believed, it is persuasively argued that whatever makes such a judgment true must have the same sort of independence from self as is credited to objective particulars in their role of outer objects, and it seems that facts alone can do this. Thus a fact is a container of a set of objects, relations and properties which gives a judgment the truth-value it has, and to say that a judgment is true is to say that there is some fact which it is about. Alternatively it has been argued that the expression 'a fact' is never an answer to the question 'What are true judgments about?' for facts are not things in the world, nor do true judgments correspond to them; instead, judgments state facts when they are true.[1] Yet the attaching of facts either to the world or to language yields an unhappy dilemma: attached to the world, facts become items to be picked out or identified, but they can be picked out only by statements that are already true; and attached to language, facts become identified with the true statements which pick them out, making facts redundant. 'Facts' remain as elusive as ever. Of course, what true statements state hardly encompass unstated facts, so that the identification of 'fact' and 'what a true statement states' seems wrong without severe qualification, ultimately admitting facts in addition to statements; and with their admission it seems essential to free the notion of 'fact' from any internal connection with belief or awareness if the occurrence of facts is to explain truth. The expedient recipe is to envisage 'the facts' as independent non-linguistic correlates of judgments and allow facts to become bearers of objectivity.

Why do we say that something is a 'fact'? The unexceptional answer is that if something is a fact it actually happened or really is so. When it is said that a man's having jaundice, being in debt or being a musician *is a fact*, what is meant is that he actually has jaundice, is in debt and is a musician, that it is not speculation, that it is so with him. It is natural to think that the fact *is* his jaundiced condition or his condition of being in debt, or of being a musician; and since his condition is something in the world, the fact, too, is something in the world. Yet this line of thought returns directly to the earlier impasse about facts and again to the question: what kind of things must facts be? It might be replied that facts are not things beyond states of affairs, for calling something a fact is an assertion of the occurrence of what was said to be the fact. So why not drop the expression 'fact' altogether and just state what happened? This tempting economy cuts facts loose from a further job they must perform. Fact-stating expressions stake two claims, that a thing *is* so and that it has been *found* to be so. By saying that such and such 'is a fact' a person conveys more than merely that his statement is true, for he also conveys that what he calls 'a fact' has been established to be the case. To assert that a man's jaundice or indebtedness is a fact is to testify to others that it has been ascertained in an appropriate and correct way to be so. This does not mean that the speaker has confirmed the matter himself or that it has been confirmed at all. By claiming it to be 'a fact' an assurance is given that confirmation has occurred, even though the assurance may be in error; and missing facts, future facts or facts unknown are projected assurances of the same sort. 'Fact' functions as a confirmation voucher.

It might be replied that this is merely one of many usages of a notoriously variable term. Ordinary discourse is flexible with regard to expressions incorporating the term 'fact' and provides a well of usage from which can be drawn with conviction alignments of 'fact' with both 'true' and 'states of affairs'. Of course in the mix of colloquial speech there is a residue of expressions in which facts figure with arguably little trace of their job of affirming confirmation: facts can be learned, believed, alleged, forgotten, regretted, and so on. But the absence of a settled usage does not invalidate the point that a philosophical interest in facts comes from a philosophical employment of the term, one in which facts are seen as the objective correlates of statements. The test is not that of mining the evidence of common usage, but whether among the usages of the term there is a role for fact-stating expressions which cannot be absorbed by expressions asserting truth or the occurrence of events. And in fact there is. When fact-stating expressions function as assurances or vouchers claiming the satisfaction of appropriate confirmation practices they cannot be replaced by terms making ontological reference or by terms of truth. For assurances of confirmation give a *reason* for affirming truth or asserting the occurrence of events. The expression 'because it is a fact' answers the question 'Why is it true?' without redundancy by explaining why assent to its truth is deserved.

There is a curious sense in which the old empiricists were right to insist that 'facts make true statements true' since a reference to the facts is indeed a reference to a good reason for asserting a statement, namely that it has passed a fair test of its truth. The mistake was to by-pass interpersonal practices and premise a reference to impersonal objects in the world; and finding only things, events and states of affairs one is left with the choice of merging 'the facts' with them or with truth-stating language. The mergers fail because facts are items of the wrong logical type to be candidates for them. Describing neither objects in the world, nor any other correlates of statements, fact ascriptions affirm the performance of well understood activities. The idea that objectivity depends on 'the facts outside' makes the mistake of assimilating practices to particulars.

The second face of objectivity does not search for external particulars beyond reach. Its invitation to think of objectivity as a part of human activity and not as a property transcending it gives the idea a welcome accessibility. The 'problem of objectivity' ceases to be the problem of identifying what lies beyond us, and becomes the problem of identifying the human actions which ensure objectiveness. It brings objectivity back to a human scale. Yet this very accessibility causes conflict by threatening the subjective–objective distinction as it is officially understood. If objectivity is something like a visible disposition, then to be objective, or to fail to be, is to conduct oneself in certain ways; the distinction between the objective and the non-objective would be drawn solely within the arena of action. And this will clash with tradition's prescription that what is subjective is 'in the mind' and that what is objective is 'outside' it. The distinction would simply be irrelevant.

How much respect does the tradition deserve? Perhaps not as much it as appears, for it cannot be said that philosophers themselves have always taken the official contrast seriously. It is honoured, often, by ignoring it; and the significant fact of its being conveniently brushed aside reveals a deeper insight into the problem. It is a manoeuvre of long standing, especially in moral philosophy, merely to pay lip service to the idea that the difference between the objective and the non-objective mirrors an inner-outer distinction. Avowals of feeling, sensations and emotions are uncontestable candidates for the application of the term 'subjective'. Yet there are other more contestable candidates, since the term is often applied to moral and aesthetic beliefs or to those we broadly call 'evaluative'. Unlike avowals they have no prima facie claim to possess the characteristics of first-person psychological statements, so a case must be made for their inclusion. The argument that, despite appearances, moral evaluations must be, or 'really are' subjective looks back in its many variations mainly to Hume, and underpins emotivism as well as its naturalistic and prescriptivist rivals. The case is disarmingly straightforward; evaluative judgments belong in the subjective class, the argument goes, because they are not open to justification or refutation by regular methods of observation and reasoning; they lack an algorithm bringing them within reason's scope. Pinning down a moral judgment as being 'subjective' is a way of objecting to the idea that it could be unrestrictedly binding; it might be true, or false, but the scope of its truth-value ranges no further than that of a person's own expressions of attitude or sentiment. Evaluations thus become agent-bound as a consequence of their premised immunity to the constraints of rationality, and the result of the strategy is the assimilation of evaluative judgments to psychological judgments. 'It is so' is absorbed by 'It is so with me.'

The strategy demonstrates that the official interchangeability of 'the subjective' and 'the mental' has been edged out by the idea that the absence of any acceptable algorithm is a force pushing to subjectivity, whereas the existence of one is a barrier against it. The contrast between the subjective and the objective ceases to be the official contrast between 'what is in the mind' and 'what is outside the mind', and is transformed into something like 'being closed to rationality binding justification' and 'being open to regular ways of settling issues about what actually is so'.[2]

Given this transformation of the official idea, the most obvious defence of ethical objectivity is the standard one that, after all, some evaluative judgments *can* be confirmed by acceptable procedures. Sustaining Mill was a deep confidence that values are in the right place, most of the time, when they are guided rightly by empirical enquiry, and that the visible consequences of actions were themselves a clear answer to moral subjectivism.[3] The importance of the 'naturalistic fallacy' lies not so much in its torpedo directed at naturalism as in its implicit recognition that Mill's position is a plausible and persuasive picture of ethics, a legitimate though wrong-headed thesis. It was not seen to be wrong because it linked objectivity with empirical methods of testing, but because it linked *moral* objectivity with them. The official subjective-objective contrast was happily passed over with the thought that in science, at any rate, objectivity and testability go together. So the way was clear to argue, cogently if incorrectly, that statements about moral values are derivable from matters of fact, despite the implied disregard of the official contrast; and to argue, as well, that moral evaluations can be rescued from subjectivity by shifting them from indicative truth-bearing moods to imperatives, and allowing them to be conclusions of valid inferences from premises of general commitment. The movement of theory along the Hume, Mill, Moore, Stevenson, Hare line of development is philosophically excusable largely because the subjective-objective difference has been prised away from an inner-outer difference. It becomes possible to argue that the objectivity of a moral belief would be sustained if it could be supported by compelling reasons of a kind that would bind anyone to it. The continuing issue is whether, in the case of moral beliefs, there could or could not be such reasons; and if there can be, what they must be like. Thus Stevenson claims that 'Rational methods can resolve ethical disagreement if and only if it is rooted in disagreement in belief'; it turns out that moral beliefs are usually a mixture of beliefs and attitudes, and where attitudes conflict rational methods defer to persuasion. What in effect defines 'disagreement in belief' is an openness, as he says, to the 'direct use of empirical and logical methods' and insofar as elements of ethical argument are open to them they remain as objective as the beliefs of science.[4] There is no question of *them* being absorbed by the sentiments or refashioned as quasi-imperative expressions of attitude.

It goes without saying, almost, that much in this positivist-inspired push to moral subjectivity and the routine defences against it is misconceived. The 'Humean' argument is not formally valid; even if a moral judgment were closed to any rational tests, this would not demonstrate that it is a psychological proposition whatever else it might do. And the identification of moral judgments with factual statements, or alternatively with prescriptive ones, arguably leaves out the essential features of moral discourse. The ambitions of this attenuated meta-ethical programme were encouraged by its perception that the real obstacle to moral objectivity was the difficulty of bringing moral beliefs within the scope of rational algorithms. The old assumption that the objectivity of values presupposes the validation of values by external items, ethical absolutes independent of the products of the mind, was ruled out as implausible at the start. How could these validating items be picked out and identified? Either they are picked out by observation, in which case there is a return to a form of naturalism, or they are decided *a priori* with the result that their externality can only be an assumption. The introduction of 'intuitions' to reveal external values was seen as a tactical way of positing the existence of values which have no other

way of making themselves apparent; they have the thankless
job of being called in when there is no room left for reason.
The significant novelty of views intermeshing with ethical
naturalism is the virtual disappearance of the idea that objectivity is, or is a product of, something 'out there'.

So there is a generous precedent for dropping a concern
with outer ontology and looking to methodology instead. If
objectivity is essential it must be accessible, a lesson not lost
on received views of scientific objectivity placing objective control within the impersonal methods of scientific practice.[5] One
may talk of the objectivity of science, but not of the objectivity
of a world beyond science. What makes a line of inquiry 'objective' is not the topics the inquiry is about, but the practices
of adjudication and confirmation with which the inquiry is
conducted. Objectivity becomes a product of proper method.
The price of objectivity, thus viewed, is a public methodology
subjecting scientific statements to the test of independent and
impartial criteria without glancing back to an inner-outer distinction. Nevertheless the commendable advance of linking objectiveness with the practice of objective methodology has its
dangers. The methodology often prescribed is geared to prevent the intrusion of subject-related bias with an overreaching
zeal. It is argued that a person's categories of thought, ideo-
logical tastes and general point of view may explain his own
opinions and account for the 'discovery' of hypotheses, but
they have no bearing on the matter of their justification. Indeed, the idea goes, they may impair it since preconceived
beliefs and expectations filtered by a point of view would undermine observation as an independent control on generalization. Laws and law-like hypotheses cannot state what is true
universally unless there are impartial restraints on the beliefs
and dispositions of individual investigators; thus, theorizing
must be checked by forcing its deductive consequences to
answer directly to neutral and theory-free observations. Observation can be interpersonal only when it is impersonal, so
scientific statements must be subject to objective control of a

sort excluding 'factors dependent upon individual biography and personality' as Kuhn described them with a rather different point in mind.

Kuhn had good reason to deplore their exclusion. He thinks that belief-laden observations need not always favour theory and sometimes theory must give way; observations are not inevitably reworked to fit the generalizations they assess. Yet there is a larger danger. Despite the welcome departure from the link-up between objectivity and outer objects, it is supposed that the more a practice becomes 'objective' the more impersonal it gets and that the main obstacle to scientific objectivity is the infusion of judgment with anything distinctive of individuals. The assumption that objective testing must as far as possible eliminate psychological and personal factors reaches back to the earlier ontological view: both aim at the maintenance of commensurability by the removal of subject-related properties, the one by refining a shared methodology and the other through a world of independent things. The interesting question is why this assumption should have been made, since it is at best a liability. To scrap the interpretive categories of an observer is to scrap his capacity to classify and describe what he observes. Observational checks are risked, not rescued, by neutrality, and attempts to eliminate the contributions of the observer without eliminating the observation are self-defeating. If the action of observing is refined to a point where it ceases to be discernible as the product of individual perceptiveness it becomes detached from any actively alert agent; it ceases, in short, to be observation.

This is hardly a fresh insight, so why was it overlooked? One answer goes back to a view about validating reasons. It is often supposed that validating reasons must be independent of the subjective beliefs of individuals if they are to be interpersonally binding; objectively valid reasons are 'outside the mind', not in some Platonic sense, but in the sense of being credited with a status external to the idiosyncratic contents of individual consciousness: they must not be subject to commitments of the will. Prompted by this supposition, objectivity is taken to be a mind-independent property precisely because validating reasons are taken to be mind-independent. With the latter theme running the argument it is understandable that qualms about the dangers of neutrality should be seen as surmountable obstacles and that a vestigial connection should be preserved between objectivity and externality.

This pursuit of purified reason neglects James's warning that the purity of reason is a myth. True enough, our validating reasons come in 'man-made wrappings' as he says. But these reasons are the best we can have because they are all we can have. By calling reasons 'subjective' James tried to shift the balance away from attempts to eliminate subject-related contributions in reasoning. It may seem a philosophical virtue to eliminate differences in ascription attributable to personal judgment, aims, values and backgrounds. But it is, James thinks, an empty one. We cannot 'weed out the human contribution' by dissociating justification and reasoning from properties that are distinctive or individuative of individual ascribers of predicates without eliminating those properties by which actions could be identified as being the actions of particular persons and hence human actions at all. James's lesson is simple enough: a judgment does not cease to be discussable, rational or justifiable merely because it is the judgment of a person.

There is little comfort to be had from the thought that at least validating reasons and hard proof escape what James vividly called 'the trail of the human serpent'. For no form of proof, even a rule-controlled proof, can ultimately eliminate the subject-related contributions of individual decisions and judgment. At the core of the idea of a rule-controlled proof is the elimination of the hazards of personal assessment. It is designed to prevent the intrusion of factors contributing to erroneous inference, hence it prohibits wrong turns a person might make by imposing stringent conditions on the options permitted. A person has only to make inferences in accord with the premises and rules, and mistakes of execution are subject to routine check by inspection. By shifting the responsibility for deciding on a conclusion *from* the unfettered judgment of a person *to* the governing rules, eccentric choices and hard decisions about cases are safely circumvented. A rule-bound proof limits one's freedom to draw the wrong conclusion.

Nevertheless if freedom is curbed by curbing decisions then some decisions must be free. There is a point in any rule-controlled proof at which decisions must rest with individual judgment. A person is prepared to allow rules of inference to determine his judgments only because he believes that the rules are of such a kind that, by letting them stand in place of his own decisions, a conclusion will follow validly or at least with rational assurance from the premises. The delegation of responsibility to a rule-governed procedure requires a prior assumption of responsibility in deciding to choose that procedure, rather than some other, as giving the desired guarantee. And this is to draw directly upon the resources of discrimination, decision and judgment. Liberty of inference is limited by rules only because of a desire to accept their constraints in the first place, and one must be satisfied about any putative rule of inference before surrendering judgment to it. The decision to do this cannot finally be a rule-constrained one. If it were, then no decisions could be constrained by rules at all, for only at the price of a regress could every decision to accept a rule of inference be a consequence of accepting a rule of inference.

So James is right in thinking that nothing can indefinitely stand in for, or replace, the human element of individual judgment. There is no question of relegating reasons of a validating kind to a domain independent of the decisions of reasoners themselves, and so no question of reasons becoming 'objective' in consequence of their possessing some special external property. Reasoning is not immune to the reactions of the reasoner, as Kuhn saw; and objectivity is not to be contrasted with that trivializing sense of subjectivity in which judgments are 'subjective' simply because they are *judgments* or expressions of the point of view of some individual agent. What matters for objectivity is not whether a person's opinions steer his judgments, but whether the opinions embodied in his judgments can survive the scrutiny of fair comment.

One may persuasively argue that to be 'fair' is to stand above interpersonal rivalries of belief and attitude, and in turn argue that objectiveness is an impersonal quality. To achieve this independence there is a standard recipe: cut back on interpersonal differences broadly attributable to biography and personality until a residue of shared ground is reached, either a common body of observations or a common fund of principles allowing a common world of discourse. The route to objectively interpersonal transactions thus goes *via* impersonal common standards guaranteeing commensurability. The motive behind the recipe is reasonable; it does seem that there have to be interpersonally shared practices of evaluation, if only because the evaluation of theories or beliefs presupposes an ability to compare them. But the recipe itself is negligent. Interpersonal transactions are necessarily bound up with the actions of individuals and are, truistically, transactions between people who will be guided by values, motives, abilities and predilections likely to spoil unanimity. Whether this happens or not is a contingent matter, and there are 'common standards of evaluation' only when there is a continuing dialogue between individuals guided in this way. The invocation of shared standards is not an *answer* to the problem of commensurability but a way of stating it; the question 'What must the common standards between all of us be like?' asks no more than the question 'What must discussions between individuals holding a mixed bag of beliefs be like?' And this is another way of saying that we determine common standards by trying to reconcile different views and interests by rational discussion.

The slogan 'commensurable because discussable' deserves respect as being, in the end, the only cogent response when pressed for neutral standards capable of resolving differences of belief. James's cautionary remarks about extrapolation are apposite here. On many occasions we compare different things, like oranges in a sack, by weighing them up against the same scale; this idea of commensurability works fine for oranges and it is tempting to let it float through to the comparison of beliefs. But beliefs are more elusive since they are held, usually, for reasons which make them compelling to people, and what compels one person may not move someone else. In measuring a belief we measure more than the belief itself, we measure it together with other supporting beliefs as Quine and Wittgenstein insist. And in the process reasoned argument presupposes a disposition to maximize understanding by adjusting across conflicting interests and views; the 'common factor' of objectiveness is a shared preparedness to keep discussion open while valuing an impartial regard for reason and evidence, leading where it will. The broad contentions of objectivity's second face thus move in the right direction. Queries about objectiveness have identifiable styles of activity and behaviour as their topics, not unidentifiable impersonal qualities. The question 'How can one be objective in one's own views?' poses no special problem beyond the question 'How can one act with reasonableness and impartiality in one's own views?' The idea is keyed to our ordinary intuitions, for it is neither novel nor controversial to say that objectiveness goes together with impartiality, disinterestedness and detachment; and to add that it goes with a respect for reason and evidence marks out the particular range of normative actions fixing the reference of the term.

Richard Rorty would not approve of at least part of this answer. He tells us that objectivity should be understood in terms of a criterion of relevance: what is 'objective' ties in with concerns that matter, whereas 'non-objective' beliefs are those rejected as being beside the point or irrelevant. They differ in degree of germainenes to a subject-matter under discussion, and to step outside objectivity is just to lapse into an unfamiliar or abnormal mode.[6] Despite its good intentions in abandoning an inner-outer view of objectiveness, Rorty's reply throws away too much. It dismisses objectivity itself by absorbing it into the category of theory-relevant items with the result that 'the objective' and 'the non-objective' lose their identities in a merger with a relevant-irrelevant distinction. Ironically this mirrors the very flaw in the link-up between objectivity and external properties which his link-up between objectivity and relevance is intended to replace, for objectivity emerges from each with no distinctive role of its own. Quite apart from trivializing objectivity by redefinition, the idea will hardly do. Today's outsider explanations sometimes become tomorrow's unexceptional stuff, so if objective and to the point tomorrow, why not objective and beside the point today? There is no plausible case for placing non-objectiveness in the family of ideas represented by irrelevance, or off-the-pointness, beyond the thought that these attributes may issue from a failure to grasp, and to heed, the constraints of argument. The contrast should be seen for what it is by pairing objectiveness with a disposition to value an impartial regard for reason and evidence. To *be* objective is to be constrained by just these values.

The emphasis on the verb 'to be' is deliberate and does much to turn this truism into something useful. It is not useful to see statements or beliefs as the basic carriers of objectivity. *People* are objective and their statements or beliefs gain whatever objectivity they have through their reception in discussion and controversy by a community respecting the constraints of rationality. Human practices are ill-served by mistaking them for linguistic or cognitive particulars, an error diverting attention from objectivity's normative home. Reasoning is a distinctively human attribute and a discussable commodity in its own right; if there are immutable rules of reason, they are there because hard work has turned them up, and the informal maxim that what hard work has done, more hard work might undo, is a warning against over-confidence. A pragmatic approach links objectiveness to a responsiveness to reasons without answering the question 'Reasons of what sort?' or endorsing the reply 'Reasons of any sort'.

If the mark of objectiveness is a respect for the constraints of reason and evidence, there is bound to be trouble once more on the subjective front. Can a person be *objective* when he makes judgments about his own feelings and states of mind? Tradition's answer is hedged with equivocation but on balance decides not. Yet is this right? That a person can be objective about the feelings and states of mind of someone else seems true; for judgments of this kind could not be made unless one has a grasp of third-person predicates, and this would presuppose an understanding of the sorts of circumstances to which they would apply and of what would count as reasons for and against their application. So if one can objectively ascribe feelings to others, why cannot one objectively ascribe them to oneself? A person judges that someone else feels pain on the evidence of behaviour and circumstances, whereas in his own case the evidence is the pain itself; and it will certainly strike the pain-experiencing agent that he is in the best possible position to be objective. It does not seem impossible that a person can have an objective view of his inner self and communicate it to others, even if this is not always done.

It might be replied that if objectiveness is understood in terms of 'being responsive to reasons' it could not apply to avowals of feeling or sensation simply because avowals are not responsive to reasons however loosely the phrase is used. The argument is that avowals are not made on the basis of anything that can be called reasons or evidence: one does not 'find out' that one is in pain or is jealous, one just has pains or is jealous; to speak of grounds for first-person statements about feelings is mistaken and the question of their being subject to reason does not arise. The objection occurs because the logic of avowals pulls in two directions. Since a person does not avow a feeling on the grounds of inference from propositions providing evidence, there is a pull towards the idea that avowals have no grounds. In the other direction there is a pull towards the idea that avowals do have grounds nevertheless. A person who avows that he feels pain when he does not says something false, so surely he says something true if he avows that he feels pain when he does; and if truth-values can be ascribed to avowals there must be grounds which can count for or against them and in virtue of which they are assigned. Both arguments pull partly to the truth, for it is right to say that avowals have a non-propositional basis and wrong to conclude that they have no basis whatever. So why not maintain the obvious and say that they are based on the evidence of feelings which an avowal purports to disclose and identify?

Of course the evidence is peculiar. A person who feels a pain can know whether his disclosures about his feelings are true or false in a way in which other people cannot. The mode of verification differs in the case of first- and third-person judgments, yet the logical uniqueness of a person's position implies nothing about the objectivity of what he chooses to relate. If the criticism that avowals of feeling stand outside objectivity is to hold it cannot rely on the premise of logical uniqueness, but on the different thought that first-person judgments of feeling are not subject to the constraints of reason and evidence.

This thought is not impressive. It is one thing to feel as one does and another to be aware of the description under which one's feelings occur. Since a person can be mistaken about the description of which his feeling is the topic, feelings and sensations must be distinguished from one's awareness of what it is that one feels or experiences, and this seems all the more the case as the range of mental predicates moves away from the transparency of 'pain' to cases where self-reflection is needed to appreciate one's state of mind. That a person may not recognize in himself the jealousy or envy attending his feelings is unquestionable despite his consciousness of those feelings. And self-deception's cure is often a matter of an objective appraisal of events shaping one's state of mind; a person who asks himself whether he is envious, or is uncertain of his jealousy, may find an answer by reviewing the evidence of his experiences and circumstances. Cases like this give a purchase on the view that a person might not know what he is feeling, just as he might not know what he is seeing, and give sense to the idea that one can, after all, find out or become aware of how one feels by relying on evidence. Any articulate judgment embodies a reliance on concepts and the management of a sophisticated ascriptive practice; it must respect standards of usage and be open to critical appraisal, and first-person avowals are no exception. The question of importance for objectiveness is whether a person is, or is not, disposed to stand back and consider what the position of his feelings really is. That rational self-reflection is in some sense 'private' is no objection; on the contrary, it tells us that objectiveness is a possible attribute of a person's inner life.

The idea that objectivity is a quality of character has the corollary that people are themselves responsible for the extent to which their actions accord with objective practice, just as they are responsible for the extent to which they are constrained by reason. In a loose sense, the objective man is the rational man. The sense is loose because rationality's scope is indeterminate in our ways of speaking, and needs the qualification that the rational man respects the reasoned criticism and the reasonable demands of others. He may or may not be the self-interested man. The rational pursuit of one's interests can clash with objectiveness by disregarding unwelcome evidence and justified opposition; equally, objectivity is not surrendered by sticking to one's interests on the strength of a reasonable case. Strong self-regard threatens objectivity, not through self-interestedness, but by overriding claims to an impartial weighing-up. And such claims we all have, for objectivity and obligation mesh together in the idea that a person has a right to expect others to honour the constraints of evidence and reasoned judgment. Hence we see objectivity as normative – we see it as a virtue.

This normative dimension links objectiveness with personal action and responsibility. The nagging issue of transforming the personal into the impersonal is a hard obstacle for theories, like Thomas Nagel's, which assume a co-dimensionality between the objective and the impersonal. Movement towards objectivity is movement 'away from the forms of perception and action distinctive of humans', as Nagel insists, and 'the pursuit of objectivity therefore involves a transcendence of the self'. If his goal of transcendence anticipates Popper's austere 'knowledge without a knowing subject' Nagel has un-Popperian reservations about the value of reaching out for it to the exclusion of all agent-centred matters; objectivity has its limits and the conflict of significance is one between extreme objectivism and a 'romanticism' in which certain subjective values are indispensable.[7] Although Nagel's liberalizing attitude acknowledges the inadequacy of accounts of experience dissociated from the accounts of experiencers, his thesis of objectivity-up-to-a-point turns on a fundamental premise shared with the extremists, that the personal dimension characterized by individual points of view is at odds with objectivity. Here we do well to heed Ramsey's maxim that conflicts between uncompromising positions often grow from a false presupposition which they hold in common.[8] The issue of substance for objectivity is not whether a view is personal or is marked by one's specific bents or position, but whether a person is prepared to open his convictions to the risks of a weighing-up by a wider community. To assert something from one's individual standpoint, from, for example, *my* point of view in which my own circumstances and their significance for me are uppermost, is not necessarily to assert something with any loss of objectiveness. It is easy enough to become a victim of those spatial metaphors which guide theorizing about objectivity, 'internal and external' or 'inner and outer'; they provide a welcome hand-hold to epistemological problems by offering a simple dichotomy of subtle power, and it is difficult to resist seeing issues in terms of a polarity which has shaped much of their historical development. But two reflections are in order. The track record of philosophical issues shaped in this way, for instance problems of mind and the external world, is a pretty poor one, and it is more than imaginable among the generic explanations of this is a root confusion of the sort James battled against in refusing to transcend the human scale. We can act in the world with understanding only by *extending* human action and understanding and not by transcending it. Extreme objectivism offers 'a universe in many editions, one real one, the infinite folio, or *édition de luxe*, eternally complete; and then the various finite editions, full of false readings, distorted and mutilated each in its own way'.[9] The irony, James thinks, is that the 'ideal limit' of an objectivist's reality has the same disability as the 'ideal limit' of a subjectivist's sense-impressions: being 'absolutely dumb and evanescent' both lie outside the limits of human articulation.

Second, quite apart from the hollow proceeds of transcendence, there is no need for it. Objectiveness is not an unattainable commodity but a disposition well within reach of rational individuals and open to explanation by explaining the springs of action. The poverty of objectivity as a product of self-transcendence is clear in its by-passing of objectivity's ethical dimension; objectiveness cannot be seen as a virtuous or desirable characteristic of people's actions if it has nothing to do with their actions at all. And a person can hardly be responsible for being or failing to be objective, or be praised or blamed for it, if objectivity is an external property ascribed independently of the desires, motivations and beliefs of any individual self. Understood in this way objectivity is an artificial concept having no application to the real world, and it is not surprising that it should prove to be so elusive. Taking a larger view of the matter, the objectivist tradition has been betrayed by an infatuation with the externalist tradition; and the exchange of its normative role for a picture of objectivity 'out there' beyond the scope of actual agents has deprived objectivism of its most cogent defences.

CHAPTER 3

A ROLE FOR OBSERVATION

The old empiricists' 'impressions' stood as bearers of truth guaranteed by an immediate confrontation with the world, leaving for us the thought that truth ascription occurs at the point of perception. But history has been unkind to the legacy. When the job of translating the idea into workable theory came under the guardianship of philosophical analysis the results were disappointing, and empiricism's retreat from the sense-datum theory is a well-documented study in the failure of strategy. With an eye on the future we do well to review some of the lessons.

In the context of the sense-datum theory it became correct but misleading to say that empirical truth is confirmed by observation; correct, because observation is ultimately decisive in settling issues of fact, but also misleading because statements of fact are proleptic, with the exception of a special class of experientially basic 'sense-datum' statements taken as the terminal bearers of truth-values. Their character was formed by the need to fasten theory to experience at a point of complete certainty, and this requires not only a test of truth but also some guarantee that the true statements emerging are true of the real world. Mathematics and logic are exempted since they are not claimed to be responsive to fact. But contingent statements must be sensitive to data if they are to be tested for truth independently of perceivers' beliefs and be authentic reports of affairs. Combining a test of truth and an anchor to the world seemed the most economical scheme, if not the only one possible, with basic control over truth-values invested in a class of referential statements having the percepts of observers as their sole topics. Being non-predictive and safe from revision by the future, sense-datum statements are secured by perceptions of the present; and if observation does not 'go beyond' given data it will give empirical truth beyond question, satisfying the demand for a firm non-inferential base in experience. Alas, the demand proved hard, and then impossible, to meet.

Standing criticism of the scheme has been both destructive and diagnostic, although the diagnoses are often too close to empiricist roots to rebuild much of use. The shift to conventionalism is one example. The trouble with sense-datum type theories, it argues, lies in the psychologistic nature of avowals of perception. Being reports on states of awareness they are not open to intersubjective testing. Hence Popper, while allowing that the experiences of a perceiving subject can causally motivate the acceptance of a basic statement, stops short of agreeing that the facts of awareness might justify accepting them.[1] By relying instead on a policy of acceptance by conventional decision he avoids 'psychologism' only to leave open a more serious question. If the acceptance or rejection of basic statements takes the shape of conventional decisions, then by what right can it be claimed that they are true of the observed world? Conventional verdicts can have no more than an *a priori* status if the algorithms of decision exclude observers' experiences altogether; and if they are not excluded, psychologism returns with a vengeance. Either way the conventionalist loses, and in the dilemma there is a moral. Final settlements by agreed decision prise testing away from what is distinctive of empiricism, the ultimate control of truth-ascription by the observation of nature.

A second diagnosis points to the thesis of incorrigibility. If the incorrigibility requirement of observation statements was eased it might be possible to rescue the original programme by replacing incorrigibility with variations on the theme of justified belief.[2] The idea has attractions. The regress of justification favours a non-inferential, certain and empirical base, but it favours without implying and it seems that no class of statements can instantiate this particular mix, so one might alter the mix by dropping incorrigibility without going against logic. And this would open an epistemic gap, one which can be closed by a fresh conception falling short of certainty and yet stronger than mere belief. The introduction of prima facie justified belief of a defeasible kind seems to fit well. Unfortunately it ensures justification but nothing else and the price to pay is high. Premises asserting justified belief at the start of the inferential pipeline of foundationalist theories give no more than conclusions about justified belief at the end. The substitution of 'justifiably' or 'warrantably' true observation statements for those previously held to be true without qualification fails to establish empirical truth at all. Behind attempts to soften a base of certainty by exchanging true statements for those asserting justified belief is the assumption, shared with an earlier empiricism, that truth is ascribed at the point of perception; and seeing that truth so ascribed is not incorrigible, it is then assumed that the most we can have are observation statements implying less than true belief. But if empirical truth is scrapped as a consequence of scrapping incorrigibility, truth drops from our beliefs about the world.

Ironically the 'justified belief' thesis is a modern version of scepticism. The ideas of justified or warranted belief cannot explain the commonplace beliefs about the world which we take as being certain. The classical argument that there is no room for empirical certainty or truth is the two-stage argument of scepticism: there is no unassailable base in the given, and there is no truth preserving inference from base to theory. By promoting a defeasible base and defeasible inferences the 'justified belief' thesis offers a re-worked version of the sceptical argument, and it is not surprising that they both have the same consequences with respect to truth. Both argue from

correct premises about the defeasibility of evidence and inference to paradoxical conclusions implying that no beliefs can
be certain, and any diagnosis must account for this oddity.
There is one which does by pointing to the foundationalist
structure itself. Within a linear model of base and inference to
higher levels, only two generic moves are possible; either to try
for truth by securing the base and strengthening the inference,
or to slacken off on both and try for something less. Logic
condemns the first and our practice condemns the second, so
something is wrong. The remedy is to set aside not only
incorrigibility, but also the foundationalist framework which
makes 'incorrigibility' such a contestable item in epistemological strategy.

The idea of inference from the given has the habit of re-
appearing in unexpected ways. Foundationalism might be defended by moving away from a phenomenalism linked with an
incorrigibility thesis to a form of realism proposing that our
commonsense view of the world can be seen as a theory for
which the data of immediate perception are evidence.[3] Such a
theory would aim to reveal those features of sensory experience
which justify our acceptance of the perceptual judgments of
commonsense which are projected from them, and since, on a
view of this kind, ordinary perceptual judgments have the
status of a realist theory, it must be possible to identify the
evidence of immediate experience independently of the commonsense judgments having them as their subjects. The thesis
attempts to salvage a distinction, fundamental to classical empiricism, between statements describing the contents of raw
experience and the realist interpretations or theories which are
supposed to go beyond them. But the distinction cannot be
maintained. Descriptions of the given are either too strict to
be faithful or too faithful to be strict. On the one hand an
account of sensory experience sufficiently strict to exclude all
reference to the theory-infused concepts of commonsense perception will be insufficiently faithful as a description of the
events perceived. It would become impossible to ascribe un-

perceived existence to objects, to make assumption about their interpersonal accessibility or to employ universal terms presupposing a history of stable predicate references, for these are part of a realist embodiment. On the other hand, if an account of sensory experience incorporates perceptual beliefs belonging to the theory itself, it may faithfully monitor experience but only at the price of becoming insufficiently strict.

It might be argued, on the contrary, that realist conceptions are not needed for true descriptions of sense-experience because such descriptions do not imply the existence of physical objects. Judgments of immediate experience could remain true even if corresponding judgments permeated with realist assumptions should be false. It this is so, then the scope of perceptual judgments is restricted to the contents of the perception of an individual ascriber; and true descriptions can be given if recourse is made to the purposive use of prefixes or locutions signalling this restriction. An agent may say how things seem to him irrespective of how they really are.

The move is unsuccessful. If the job of indicating the judgments' special status falls on the locution or prefix, the job of description falls on the sentences recording the ascriber's perceptions. And such sentences cannot be open to ascriptions of truth if they are closed to realist concepts. The ascriber must be apprised of the special status of his judgment and of the role of the locutions employed in characterizing it; he must take it to be an avowal and not a judgment of a wider kind, and be under no obligation to report things as they are but only as they seem to him. Indeed an entailment-breaking use of 'seems', in this context, acknowledges an awareness of the commitment. Yet it is not possible that a person should be in a position to attach the required sense to this idea, one in which the suspension of this obligation is understood, and also fail to attach a sense to the thought of things being so irrespective of how they seem to him. And insofar as sense is attached to this distinction, one is committed to a grasp of realist concepts in describing one's experiences.

Why should views faithful to the founding principles of the old empiricists finish in such disarray? Perhaps the answer is simply that they are too loyal to break away boldly at key points. Yet there is a notable exception. Quine has no such inhibitions and his break-away points are easily identifiable: the rejection of foundationalist structures in favour of a holistic structure, his repudiation of the idea of pushing back to raw-data descriptions of experience, and his recognition of the need to anchor theory to the world without relying on a mirroring relation of correspondence. Yet he affirms empiricism with his uncompromising remark 'Whatever evidence there *is* for science *is* sensory evidence'.[4]

James and Quine share so much in their holistic attitudes that the deep division between their humanist and behaviourist approaches to the issue of observation is all the more significant. The important question is whether Quine's behaviourist account of observation can preserve the 'human contribution' which shapes James's side of the issue.

Quine proposes that a sentence is an 'observation sentence' if on any occasion its truth-value would be agreed to by any, or nearly any, number of people of a speech community witnessing the occasion; they will give similar verdicts in the presence of the same causal impingements on their sensory nerve-endings.[5] This is attractive as an alternative to a base for observation in 'awareness', Quine's summary term for the activities of consciousness and what goes with them. Yet the crucial question of how 'observation sentences' can be picked out from sentences of other kinds is given an answer that hardly inspires confidence. On Quine's criterion an observation sentence can be identified only on the assumption that the witnesses on the occasion of uttering the sentence are subject to shared sensory stimulations; the sentence must draw assent when this is true. If this assumption about shared impingements is taken to be true as an inference from, roughly, a theory or hypothesis about the interaction between behaviour and environment, as it must be, we allow theory to call the shots in identifying what is to count as an observation sentence. Remembering, as Quine holds, that it is the job of an observation sentence to give evidence for theories and hypotheses, or to give varying measures of truth-control over them, the hypothesis of interaction backing an inference about shared stimulations cannot be supported or controlled by appealing to observation sentences which presuppose its truth. Yet, indeed, it is. As a result 'observation sentences' suffer a circular introduction; the hypothesis needed to identify them must be assumed to be correct before any observation sentences can be picked out, yet some observation sentences must be picked out before they can attest to the correctness of the hypothesis.

Why, then, stick with observation sentences? Clearly Quine saw the trouble. Circularity objections never bothered him much and can be shelved if the capacity of a scheme to explain and order experience commends itself to us better than any other, even if it involves a *petitio*.[6] Since there is reason to think that James himself would have sympathized, the source of their doctrinal difference must be somewhere else. One might complain that shared stimulations cannot stand-in for shared observations because information about sameness of retinal irradiations and sentence output can give at most information about constancy of stimulation and response, and no information about a perceived world. True, no doubt, and damaging to Quine, yet not a pointer to the difference between him and James. More relevant is the thought that if 'response' is tied closely to the idea of consensus, in the way it is by Quine, shared or interpersonal concepts and beliefs win a mentalistic foothold to the detriment of the theory; and if they do not, then the ascription of truth by way of communal assent loses credibility.

The main issue is whether 'awareness' has any role at all. Quine's dismissive reply 'awareness be hanged' is cold comfort to a philosopher like James who has awareness etched on his soul. The short way to deal with awareness is to treat an observer as a black box with an input of stimulations and an output of sentences, and this Quine does.[7] It is a fatal move, for it fails to face up to the fact that the 'output sentence' is not just a sentence but is an utterance by a person. If just a sentence, it would fail as a sentence distinctively expressing an observation, for there is no observation without an observer and no observer without an observant person; the observation is his or her product. The most decisive refutation of some postulated occurrence of an observation would be to show it has not been made by anyone: and in Quine's case there is only a stimulus and a response, leaving the model consistent with the hypothesis that the output sentence was not uttered by a person at all. Since an observation report implies in the strictest sense the activities of a perceiving agent, the 'black box' idea cannot rescue things here.

No wonder that James insisted on a place for people. Without them testing stops altogether. So why make Quine's rash move? Behind the issue is a worry about privacy and its consequences, since the intentionality of observers' claims involves a troublesome subjectivity and a mentalism unassessible by a witnessing public. The advantage of focusing on spoken sentences in company with multiple assent in a common stimulus situation is the achievement of visible agreement against a background of measurable input. It gives us 'the minimum verifiable aggregate' and hence, as Quine says, an openly identifiable basis for judgment with no 'appreciable fallibility', one strong enough to act as a check on theory even if a temporary check.[8] 'Observation sentences' emerge with two roles and the question of whether they are consistent is a real one. On the one hand they are arbiters of theory and, on the other, open to rejection if they conflict with theory deeply entrenched. These different functions may be reconciled, Quine thinks, by the supposition that present assent is subject to future withdrawal; theory is controlled on a given occasion with the possibility of revision later on. This pragmatic thought seems sharply opposed to non-Quinean empiricism's vision of irrevisable basic statements. Yet the two schemes grow from the same motive of securing an empirical base immune to surprise and retraction, even though there is another unshared and opposing motive which Quine's pragmatism dictates, namely that no base is immune in this way. Hence the strain of conflicting interests making up what is, essentially, a hybrid epistemology.[9] There is a pull both towards and away from orthodox empiricism, resulting in two stories. Observation sentences in their 'nearly infallible' role decide theory, so they must be firmly true when close to stimulations. Here the pull to tradition. In their other role scientific theory guides the selection of observations and may take precedence over them when established on a wide explanatory front, so even if close to stimulations their 'firmness' is potentially revisable. Here the pull to pragmatism. Considered separately each story is cogent, the first is something like a classical foundations theory seen through behaviourist spectacles, and the second a coherence theory embodying Neurath's parable of the boat.[10] Quine's caution leads to the decision to hold on to both stories in the conviction that the first story is needed to fasten statements truly to the world, even if the second is a more realistic account of scientific practice. The result approximates to that graft between foundationalism and coherence which James saw as a reversion to error, and the breakaway from orthodox empiricism is incomplete.

Quine's decision to run the two stories together encourages the mistaken idea that observation and the assignment of truth must coincide. By taking observation sentences as determinants or partial determinants of truth at the level of theory one is committed to take them to be true at their point of origin, if the first story is right. The second story has no fixed anchorage for truth; truth emerges as a product of intelligent adjustment in the interests of explanatory coherence tempered by other virtues of method. And this has its dangers, as James found out to his cost. Without the first story's anchorage, theory might float freely off the world. Seeing this, Quine built an anchor to the world into observation sentences. If he had followed Popper in accepting concurrence alone as a measure for truth (or something near to it) there would have been no case for a purchase on the facts. Popper held to the idea that truth-control over theory is determined by the singular observation statements implied, and he exchanged a base in awareness for a base in convention. This escaped the problems of a terminus in sensation but had the serious disadvantage of relinquishing the guarantee, which a base in sensation gave, that the statements in question applied to the witnessable events of nature. Quine avoided this trap by his addition of a common stimulus requirement putting a speaker in a position to claim that he is assenting to, or dissenting from, queries about physical reality. He sees this asset as providing an entry into language free from the biography of speakers and as doing this by a visible connection, 'for observation sentences are precisely the ones we can correlate with observable circumstances of the occasions of utterance or assent independently of variations in the past histories of individual informants'.[11] Shared 'impingements' on the sensory surfaces, in the presence of a common source of physical stimulation and in close proximity to utterances, provide a causal link between the witness and the world. The 'causal closeness' of output sentences to input stimulations ensures that observation sentences have the world as their topics.

The idea is ingenious but needs sifting. We may, Quine says, 'talk explicitly in terms of causal proximity to sensory receptors' and look for an agent 'exposed to externally determinable stimulatory forces as input and spouting externally determinable testimony about the external world as output'.[12] Why not, alternatively, redescribe this as looking for a reporting observer who is on the spot at the time? Quine would disapprove mainly because of the hidden mentalistic reference; as with statements, propositions, beliefs and meanings, 'observing' needs translation into openly testable terms. But the caveat disappears once we are untroubled by mentalism. Ordinary talk can capture the gist of Quine's remarks by saying that when a man is in a position to say what he sees in the world, and does so, this is an important and valuable fact, for it separates his statements from other statements having a dissimilar provenance. And 'provenance' is what observation statements give by certifying that a witness observed a bit of the world under a certain description at a given time and place. The question of whether it is the role of observation sentences to give true descriptions, or just descriptions with a distinctive provenance, never arose for Quine. He tried to pack both functions into observation's job while avoiding awareness in the process, and too much was packed in to ask whether a sentence can have the world as its reference without prejudice to its truth-values. Here we do well to keep independent issues apart. Having noted that in testing we seek statements that are both true and true of the world, we should satisfy the conjuncts by different routes. To anchor a statement in experience is not to anchor it in truth. It is to establish it as the verdict of an observing person, leaving open the disposition of its truth-values.

Once we accept that the truth of a witness's statement is bound up with factors of biography, inference and belief reaching beyond the occasion of observation, the idea that truth is given at the point of perceptual contact ceases to be credible, and it becomes plausible to ask why observation should matter at all. It matters because eye-witness reports prevent an epistemology from detaching itself from the world by documenting the act of observation itself. The person who says he saw, for instance, the victim at the moment of his being shot, makes a claim both about his impressions and about his own biography; he was there, in a position to see and did see, an event he describes in some such way. One may question the details of his story ('One shot or two?') as well as his credentials to tell it ('Could you see from where you were?'), and his biography establishes or refutes him as a witness without commenting on the veracity of the story. We can credit him as being a witness without crediting his story with truth, and vice versa. The

distinction is an unexceptional but important pointer to a larger lesson: 'observation' is not a process which gives truth to
statements but one which gives them a right to apply to an
observed world; it attests to the conditional 'If true, then true
of the world' leaving the antecedent 'if' as a matter for decision. To fasten a statement to the observed world is necessarily to fasten it to the verdict of some observer, and to fasten
it to the world is not to make it true. Eye-witness reports secure
empirical authenticity but they remain discussible and the
route to truth lies elsewhere.

The lesson is an old one freshly remembered, for the old
empiricists appreciated that truth about the world presupposes
contact with the world. They confronted observation reports
with experience by narrowing down their descriptive content
to a point of exact match between basic descriptions and raw
data. Although much was wrong here, the project correctly
assumed that it was the job of an observation statement to
report the verdict of an observer on the spot at the time. Thus
Neurath insisted on the inclusion of a biographical element in
protocol sentences specifying the circumstances of their origin.[13] Yet anxieties about truth transformed what was essentially a biographical reference certifying the occurrence of
observation into a perceptual statement describing true
impressions, and the description was pushed too far. Motivated
by the belief that it must be narrowed down to a point of
incorrigibility, it was taken beyond significantly describable
limits by attaching its elements to those of private awareness.
The mistake was not only the notorious one of seeking security
in the data of impressions, but a more serious one. For the
reduction of the descriptive content had the effect of by-passing
vernacular descriptions of the world. Descriptions characteristic of realism vanished into those of the sense-datum theorists'
unattainable ideal and the result was a data base incapable of
articulate expression. Quine, especially, steered clear of this
and added a liberating insight to correct the downward drift.
The topics of observation reports must range over the contents

of experience prosaically stated, for example, 'This shard was embedded 10 mm below the layer of ashes in the trench.' As in Quine's analogy, observation verdicts like 'The stuff has gone green' are base blocks supporting and supported by an arch of sentences theoretically fitting together and are often 'skipped as the theory becomes second-nature'.[14] By-passed by unspoken assent they evade the limelight too easily and conceal that just such mundane events as an observer's reporting the coincidence of a pointer with a point on a scale, or a change of colour, capture the position of description at the base of testing. If phenomenalism pushes description too far in the direction of loss of sense, realism may push it too far in the direction of the idiom of theory with the loss of vernacular expression. But it need not, as Quine notes, and we expect from theory implications of the order of Quine's commonplace base-blocks. He saw them as eventually taking the shape of utterances closest to the non-verbal stimulations eliciting them, thus circumventing awareness. The latter motive apart, the idea revealed that theory is connected to the world at a vernacular level.

Vernacular expressions of observation rely on realist assumptions since description distinctive of the world presupposes realist conceptions of the independence and endurance of objects, their accessibility to different observers and their possession of causal powers. Yet it is a thesis of traditional empiricism that conceptions of this kind cannot be solicited directly from perception; they are products of inference from the given and where there is inference there is room for truth-defeating error. Even if this objection were sound it would be less than germaine since the demand for realist description is a requirement for verifiability rather than for verification. Moreover the truism that there is no describing without describing counts against it. Experience self-consciously heeded can be described 'phenomenally', so to speak, but only against a background of realist conceptions. Observers cannot make their experiences intelligible to themselves and to others unless they can see them for the most part as experiences of a physical world; for they cannot think of themselves as being in a frame of mind in which there is no place for realistically conceived events without also having a conception of what is individuative of such a frame of mind, namely the exclusion of just such events. The language of phenomenalism presupposes a capacity to express experiences in realist terms.

More serious is a standing concern about truth. Provenance may show that vernacular verdicts of observation have the world as their topics but observation is silent about their truth-values. Yet we still seek them since theory needs a base in truth, however attained. Standard practice in testing prescribes that truth-values are assigned within a hypothetico-deductive framework having the aim of placing an observer in a position to confront the phenomena to be observed with a singular statement under test. Given that there is no falsification of theory without truth somewhere along the line, notably at the level of an observation verdict, testing must assume that some verdict is unassailable if it is to score hits on hypotheses. Yet this assumption seems impossible to make, if only for the reason that the implications of an observation verdict are unsteady. Consistency-restoring conjectures freely replacing elements in the framework can save hypotheses from refutation. And among the replaceable elements are observation statements themselves, a fact which underlines the vulnerability of any truth-values temptingly assigned to them. So the situation is serious. The idea of a truth-value base in vernacular expression seems inadequate because descriptions in the common idiom act as falsifiers only in the light of interpretation. They are themselves in the dock along with interpretive theory and any 'firmness' is diffused throughout knowledge. Whether an observation inferentially linked to a generalization at issue is within the range of cases to which the predicate 'true' applies would have to be *decided*. One way of doing this is to decide about the observation verdict by deciding about the hardness of background knowledge taken as true, and this may call for restrictions on the admission of conjectures impairing falsification. The standing conception of essential background knowledge embraces a bulk of scientific theory used as an uncontested fulcrum for assessing hypotheses under test. Let it be reported after observation that a quantity of specified stuff weighs 50 grammes; it must then be decided whether this verdict would conflict with other judgments taken as part of essential background knowledge hardened as much as can be. But a hardened background seems an elusive ideal, given that there are indefinitely many ways of adjusting its stock of beliefs to accommodate dissent from the verdict. Firmness fails if no constituents are irreplaceable and none seem to be. If neither hypotheses nor observations, nor any other element is closed to revision and if no revision is unassailable, the testing enterprise seems subject to an inescapable dilemma. Unless some statements are taken to be firmly true, testing cannot be decisive; but if none are immune to challenge, none can be taken as firmly true.

The quandary is partly a product of pragmatism's take-over of the hypothetico-deductive model; the *modus tollens* refutations of naive falsificationism disappear in the elasticity of a holistic system prescribing an egalitarian vulnerability. Hence Neurath's boat. But an input of truth-values is needed even if no statement is immune to withdrawal however strong its claims to retention, so it is tempting to loosen up on truth and exchange 'immunity to withdrawal' for a more mobile epistemic notion not implying certainty, and to fall back on a degree of credibility. The problem is not peculiar to pragmatism and has an analogue in foundationalism's updated replacement of incorrigibility by justified or warranted belief. The outcome is similar in both cases. Inputs of credibility give credibility alone at the end; there is no magical adjustment capable of squeezing certainties or the like from probabilities and a pragmatic system can transmit credibility but cannot transmute it into anything better. Pragmatism's virtue of using observation to tie theory to the world without prejudging verification seems possible only at the cost of a permissive conception of truth.

James would not have agreed. One of the delights of Jamesian pragmatism is its capacity to pursue unpromising lines and come up with riches at the end. Not that they will satisfy everyone, and James himself must have been discouraged by his ultimate lack of success in giving truth a clear title while steering between absolutism and relativism. When he remarked that we call something true 'for human reasons' he could hardly have been wrong, so why the need for emphasis? His obvious target is the rather diffuse thought that truth is 'out there', an ideal compelling to a Platonic turn-of-mind and sought by the intellectualizing rationalism he opposed. But there are other targets closer to home. Peirce can be credited with the idea that truth is the long run goal of science, in theory if not in the actual aims of its practitioners. By pursuing the self-correcting methods of science divergent views, given sufficient time, will gradually converge on a point of consensus. And Peirce says that this alone is what he calls truth.[15] Peirce is sufficiently wary to avoid trapping himself in a commitment to scientific progress, and what looks like prophecy turns out to be argued faith; but his hope of truth at the end of inquiry is nevertheless real. It is a matter of sticking with proper method and carrying investigations far enough.

On the other side of the coin is Kuhn's reply that in science no movement carries us closer and closer to the truth; indeed there is no such goal, not even 'a process of evolution *toward* anything'.[16] There can be no convergence, not because there is nothing we might call 'progress', but because there is no end to converge upon. Both the 'convergence' and the 'non-convergence' thesis run counter to James's message that truth is elusive because people often fail to see how things fit together. Truth lies neither in the future nor wherever one likes, but in its present-tense usefulness. In the Jamesian vocabulary what is 'useful' can usually be exchanged for what is 'satisfactory' or what is 'good in the way of belief'; all refer to the end-product of a process in which new bits of information, perceptual or otherwise, are fitted into an 'older stock of truths with a minimum of modification'. And the latter is important, for an ill-fitting new bit can be assimilated by re-shaping or throwing out older ones, if its incorporation gives greater coherence and sense to the whole and hence greater satisfaction or usefulness to us:

> The individual has a stock of old opinions already, but he meets a new experience that puts them to a strain. Somebody contradicts them; or in a reflective moment he discovers that they contradict each other; or he hears of facts with which they are incompatible, or desires arise in him which they cease to satisfy. The result is an inward trouble to which his mind till then had been a stranger, and from which he seeks to escape by modifying his previous mass of opinions. He saves as much of it as he can, for in this matter of belief we are all extreme conservatives. So he tries to change first this opinion, and then that (for they resist change very variously), until at last some new idea comes up which he can graft upon the ancient stock with a minimum of disturbance of the latter, some idea that mediates between the stock and the new experience and runs them into one another most felicitiously and expediently.
>
> This idea is then adopted as the true one. It preserves the older stock of truths with a minimum of modification, stretching them just enough to make them admit the novelty, but conceiving that in ways as familiar as the case leaves possible.[17]

The link between coherence, or what might be called the organizing capacity of a system, and the ideas of utility and satisfaction is indicative of the shift away from Peirce. Although both philosophers emphasized the consequences of belief, James saw that the logical implications of belief, the focus of Peirce's attention, cannot by themselves account for changes in thought and action; the implications must weigh with an agent enough to move him to act, and for this some bait is needed in the form of causal consequences which an agent finds satisfying or useful to himself. 'Satisfaction' emerges as James's tradeword for the psychological pay-off of a coherent set of beliefs maximizing a grip on experience. We say, James tells us, that one theory solves the problem of reconciling new data with received beliefs more satisfactorily than some other theory, 'but that means more satisfactorily to ourselves, and individuals emphasize their points of satisfaction differently'.[18] The echo of relativism is clear in this 'relativizing' of benefits; different theories can satisfy differently because different backgrounds have different demands, expectations and prior beliefs and individuals too may vary in their perceptions of what is useful or worth having. James is less interested in 'relativism' as a philosophical issue than as a visible manifestation of changes and shifts in belief across cultures and times; to 'weed out the human contribution' is stubbornly to oppose obvious facts about human differences. Like any other element of nature they have to be lived with, and in philosophy, taken into account. A strategy for truth must acknowledge and try to reconcile them.

Pragmatism's commitment to an ongoing process of change starts with the unexceptional idea that people are not immune to the impact of fresh events on their current beliefs and the redistribution of truth-values this must bring. Since our grip on the world is a function of our current beliefs, what is satisfying or useful *now*, may not have been earlier and may not be later on; as James says, 'To a certain extent, therefore, everything here is plastic', a reminder of Neurath's and Quine's point. And plasticity begins with an awareness of the utility of truth; we *could* revise the truths we accept, but we do not if they are frozen into a background too solid to thaw without drastic results. The following passage is from James's discussion in 'Humanism and Truth':

> Moses wrote the Pentateuch, we think, because if he didn't, all our religious habits will have to be undone. Julius Caesar was real, or we can never listen to history again. Trilobites were once alive, or all our thought about the strata is at sea. Radium, discovered only yesterday, must always have existed, or its analogy with other natural elements, which are permanent, fails.

In all this, it is but one portion of our beliefs reacting on another so as to yield the most satisfactory total state of mind. The state of mind, we say, sees truth, and the content of its deliverances we believe.[19]

Here, as elsewhere, James relies on the disjunctive argument 'either I believe *this*, or I scrap the better part of knowledge' as a constraint on the acceptance or rejection of belief. The criterion is both psychological and rational. The rejection of a given belief will be out of the question if its consequences mean changes in one's overall scheme of beliefs which are too disruptive to sustain a satisfactory adaptation to experience. The thought is Quine's almost as much as James's. In James's hands advantages are set against disadvantages, usefulness against what is useless. And this gives a clear sense to his italicized idea that '*The true is the name of whatever proves itself good in the way of belief, and good, too, for definite assignable reasons.*'[20] A belief is good in the way of belief if we grant that the alternative of chaotic belief is bad. A belief is true on the grounds of reasons which cannot be questioned without questioning other beliefs essential to a coherent picture of the world; and with a background premised as true, the truth of the belief follows. As James remarks, 'consistency is the most imperious claimant' and the disjunctive argument can be as truth-preserving as any valid argument. Of course, valid inference is content to push along the pipe-line whatever truth, or rubbish, is shoved in at the start, and the question is whether the contents it pushes through are true to begin with. James's answer is unconventional, at least by foundationalist standards. There is no fountainhead of truth, no external source to be tapped by correspondence to the real. We enter a world complete with things and theories – it is a going concern and we are part of it. We do not start from scratch, and the discernment of truth is essentially a process of sifting, adjusting and revising both observations and the practical and theoretical paraphernalia of ideas acquired in the learning of one's own culture.

Largely for this reason James could allow with equanimity that perception is inseparable from our own filtering views: 'Take our sensations. *That* they are is undoubtedly beyond our control; but *which* we attend to, note, and make emphatic in our conclusions depends on our own interests'; 'we receive in short the block of marble, but we carve the statue ourselves.'[21] His insistence that sensations 'are neither true nor false; they simply *are*' repudiates the thought that truth is given at the point of perceptual contact. The theory-ladenness of perception is no obstacle to truth if it is not perception's business to supply truth. Verification is a process, of which perception is only one essential element. Claims about the experienced world must lead to sensible experiences *somewhere*, he emphasizes, if they are to be genuinely about the experienced world and testify to encounters with it. But the assessment of truth-claims occurs in the process of mediation between incoming encounters and standing opinion.

The old empiricists faced the problem of reconciling the stability of truth with a background of continuing change, and the answer naturally enough suggesting itself was to take truth as a fixed constant in a field of variable candidates for it. James's work is remarkable in its reversal of the formula; there is no fixed constant of truth, and the variable candidates may each be true. To think otherwise, James believed, would be irresponsible both to philosophy and to the facts of nature. He saw that an explanation of 'true belief' narrows down to a focus on the believers themselves; there are not two separate issues, one of explaining the truth of a belief and the other of explaining why people stick to some beliefs and modify or set aside others. There is a single issue in which the explanations coincide, summed up in James's slogan 'The reasons why we call things true is the reason why they *are* true.'[22] Of course there is great strength in the objection that both P and not-P cannot be true. The point might be evaded by saying that, at any rate, P in L_1 and not-P in L_2 is all right provided that 'true' means 'true in some L'. Since this is suspiciously close to 'true for us' it is necessary to see that James's rendering of 'true for us' is not 'true in some L' but more like 'true by a pragmatic process in any L': 'Any idea that helps us to *deal*, whether practically or intellectually, with either the reality or its belongings, that doesn't entangle our progress in frustrations, that *fits*, in fact, and adapts our life to the reality's whole setting, will agree sufficiently to meet the requirement. It will hold true of that reality.'[23] James envisaged the process of pragmatic adjustment as an algorithm which people of diverse interests and outlooks could share as a means of achieving a view which best fitted their own requirements in adapting themselves to their experiences. The idea of a constant gives way to a 'pragmatic continuity' across different views, each capable of revising the other. Like 'a rope in which each fibre leads a separate life', as James says, one field of belief will overlap or impinge upon another and the interchange of criticism will, or may, leave them both altered. There is no fibre running continuously through the rope and no single strand as a final goal. True belief is belief assimilable in a background, false belief is not; and the law of the excluded middle is respected in the contrast between assimilable and non-assimilable belief.

By offering a conception of truth tied to actual practice rather than to a theoretical ideal James is set on a collision course with epistemologies balking at a pluralistic notion of truth. It is a measure of James's innovation that he should reply by explaining *why* one might balk. Through learning and experience, he thinks, it becomes second nature to look for consistency as far as we can, and to attain it by pragmatic adjustments which profit our lives. Heeding our habits, we may think that if consistency within a given background of observation and belief is a pragmatic measure of truth, why not have consistency common to all backgrounds as a theoretic measure of truth? By extending the idea of consistency within a system, which generates a pluralistic version of truth, we can postulate a monadic version of consistency across systems giving not 'truths' but truth absolutely. The mistake, James replies, is to follow our impulses too far into theory and deny satisfaction in the pursuit of an illusory ideal; we indulge our speculative inclinations and we extrapolate heedless of the facts. In this way 'the form of inner consistency is pursued far beyond the line at which collateral profits stop'. If the evidence for 'absolute truth' ranges no further than truths 'true within those borders of experience', then the extrapolation is no more secure than the evidence itself and 'the purely theoretic criterion of truth can leave us in the lurch as easily as any other criterion'; they are 'in the same boat'.[24]

James's dogged refusal to be deflected from the diversity of human perspectives was bound to clash with tidy theorizing. There is no prospecting for final certainties simply because 'no point of view can ever be *the* last one'. The message is clear enough, but the loose ends are too. He did not want a permissive sort of truth identifiable with mere credibility or probability; 'truth as one sees it' is not the same as 'credibility as one sees it' and it is an understandable mistake in reading James to confuse the two. If he had merged them in the interests of moderating the opposition James's task would have been appreciably easier, for it is not an affront to theory to argue that there are lots of different credibilities or probabilities because there are lots of different points of view. James is the last person to brush aside the common conviction that truth means more, even if what it means is unexplained. His own explanation that true beliefs adapt us best to changing circumstances prescribes what truth *is* without escaping the predicament which all pragmatist theories must reckon with: if the plasticity of the system ensures the possible revisability of all its statements then 'truth' must permissively yield to credibility; and if more is wanted, some statements must be unassailably entrenched.

Quine's philosophy testified to the difficulty of balancing an honest respect for truth against an honest respect for change. His shunting between 'no appreciable fallibility' and 'openness to revision' resulted in a strained compromise between elasticity and rigidity, and gave a split epistemology unsatisfying to pragmatists and foundationalists alike. James's attempt to extract truth from holistic adjustments sought more than they could give and was equally unsatisfying. He thought that truth could be the product of a system embracing the possible revisability of any of its elements without any independent source of certainty. So he impatiently answers the objection that certainty somewhere beyond a pragmatic algorithm for truth is necessary, 'But is this not the globe, the elephant and the tortoise over again?'[25] One might answer yes, without being the absolutist critic James addressed, for there is a sense in which the criticism is right and it has little to do with spuriously timeless truths. The clamour for them is a demand for 'independence' which echoes in epistemology from Achilles to Popper, a demand satisfied by building into methods of justification items like intuitions, conventions, self-evident principles and external realities, depending on one's philosophical bent. Wittgenstein appreciated the value of independence as much as anyone and saw that if the idea of independence was to be of any use in underwriting truth-claims then 'independent' must read as 'independent of *any* methods of justification'. This is not a thought which James or Quine would have shared.

CHAPTER 4

CERTAINTY AND HUMAN ACTION:
WITTGENSTEIN

Thoughts about truth are apt to be confined by two idealized models of justification. The first is the linear model, in which predicate ascription on a given occasion is justified by inference from something else supported, in turn, by inference from something further. Its virtue is the avoidance of circularity and its problem is to bring the line of inferences to a halt. But truth-transmission is empty without a truth-initiating base and no such base is part of the linear structure itself. The options remain of looking outside it for intimations of truth or of envisaging the structure of justification in different terms. The second is the coherence model which offers justification freed from the idea of a terminus. Its virtue is the avoidance of linear regress, since the truth of a statement arises from a compatible fit within a systematic set of other statements. And this is also its problem, for it runs the risk of a circularity in which statements under test figure in the support of the other statements used in testing them. Invariably it invites the objection that coherence of fit gives justification only if some statements within the system are independently assessable.

Both models share the same disadvantage of cutting themselves off from truth unless augmented by the additional resources of epistemological theory. Self-evidence or incorrigibility might aid the linear model, and the assignment of truth-values by correspondence prior to consistency screening might help coherence; or one may forego truth and settle for warranted assertibility. All of these steer back to foundation-alism as regional varieties and inherit its defects.

More promising is the general notion that control over truth is exercised by a mixed background of people's beliefs, observations and practices. The thought belongs to James. Neurath, with Quine following him, shaped it into a no-entrenchment thesis coupled with the elimination of awareness. Although the result was unworkable epistemology there is something right about the generic idea, for truth-ascription requires a coherent network of beliefs and practices as well as access to data. This rough notion was given shape and content in Wittgenstein's last work. Refusing Popper's invitation to conventionalism and Quine's to behaviourism, Wittgenstein contributed a funda-mental insight: the philosophy of evidence and justification cannot be grasped by focusing on evidence and justification alone, for it is inadequate unless it explains the non-evidential basis of our beliefs and this essentially involves people and their practices.

In outline, the strategy of *On Certainty* combines a thesis about evidence, a thesis about epistemological status and a thesis about priority. The thesis about evidence tells us that within 'our picture of the world' there are two broad classes of beliefs or propositions, those which are grounded – we may use standard procedures of testing and reasoning in support of their truth – and those which we accept without grounds, justification or proof. The thesis about epistemological status holds that grounded beliefs are corrigible and open to the possibility of doubt, although a special class of ungrounded or 'groundless' beliefs are taken to be certain and beyond doubt, possessing the informativeness of empirical beliefs and the entrenchment of logical truths. The thesis about priority prescribes that beliefs of the first grounded sort are logically parasitic on those of the second ungrounded sort, such that there can be no grounded beliefs in probabilities unless some beliefs are accepted as certain without grounds.

Traditional epistemology sharply separates the explanations

of why a belief is certain from the explanation of why individuals accept it as being certain, the former accounting for the
truth of a belief in terms of the reasons or grounds which justify
it and the latter accounting at most for the causes of assent to
it. It is important to appreciate the unorthodox nature of Wittgenstein's refocusing of this view. What is needed, he thinks,
is an explanation of the factors constraining assent to entrenched beliefs and of the actions of ascribers underlying their
entrenchment. It strikes him that the question of why entrenched beliefs like Moore's are certain, and the question of
why language users sharing a practice hold them to be certain,
are connected in a radical way. The explanation of why such
beliefs are *held* to be certain is the explanation of why they *are*
certain; there is no explanation of the certainty of ungrounded
beliefs beyond one accounting for the activity of 'standing fast'
with them. As he sees the matter, the very possibility of anything called 'scientific method' is dependent upon this. The
implications for epistemology are serious. The ultimate explanation of the certainty of our deeply entrenched beliefs is found
in human action, hence their certainty is not based on anything that is true or false or is itself 'grounded'. When we push
back reasons, evidence and grounds for a belief we come to
beliefs which we will not give up even though we do not use
reasoning, evidence and grounds to justify their certainty. The
shift is radical in theory: by placing human behaviour at the
foundation of judgment, questions of justification finally become questions of the constraints which shape our actions.

If Wittgenstein is right, the line between conviction and
truth must be redrawn without sacrificing reason's role in the
root-source of certainty. We do not, Wittgenstein says, provide
reasons for the truth of 'groundless' beliefs in the form of evidence for them, nevertheless we do adduce reasons for their
entrenchment in the form of constraints on action. Some beliefs
are entrenched and some are not and this, Wittgenstein thinks,
is not an arbitrary matter. An impressively large chunk of *On
Certainty* is devoted to demonstrating that the entrenchment of

a belief can be a matter for reasoned decision even if its truth or falsehood is not. By shifting the area to which rational discussion is appropriate away from the justification of entrenched beliefs and into the different area of the explanation of our actions in refusing to repudiate them, his redrawing of the line preserves the role of rationality at the level of fundamentals. Central to Wittgenstein's position is his distinction between 1) the assignment of truth-values to a belief on the strength of evidence for and against it, and 2) the explanation of the actions of ascribers in refusing to abandon or to accept a belief; and that although 2) is independent of the evidence figuring in 1), nevertheless 1) is dependent on 2). Hence it is possible to argue, as Wittgenstein does, that even if the provision of evidence or reasons for a belief comes to an end in our action of 'standing fast' so there can be no question of demanding further grounds, there is still a question open to rational discussion of why on a particular occasion one *does* 'stand fast'. And here he forcefully makes the point that decisions about the entrenchment of a belief are regulated by considerations of consistency and coherence, for a person's conceptual background or view of the world must hang together connectedly. These decisions are neither arbitrary nor outside reason for there are, as he illustrates repeatedly, good reasons for refusing to budge.

This bare sketch needs to be fleshed out. James shared much with Quine although even more with Wittgenstein and the common roots of doctrine and attitude grow deeply in *On Certainty*. As James thought, all ascriptive practice is infused with a way of seeing the world, an outlook reflecting a form of living and acting; it is there in our life, a constituent of nature as much as are surroundings of geography, climate and natural resource fixing our condition; yet it is subject to manipulation and change. Importantly, the assessment of our beliefs depends upon this acquired fund of 'beliefs in stock'. With Jamesian insight Wittgenstein picks up the thought. The 'inherited background against which I distinguish between true and false' is a condition of our having intelligible beliefs and forms my 'picture of the world', a comprehensive 'system', as he says, making their justification possible; it is 'the element in which arguments have their life'.[1]

The pragmatist leanings behind Wittgenstein's anti-foundationalism appear in the importance he attaches to an inherited conceptual system as a presupposition of testing. We are invited to envisage a background broadly dominated by beliefs of two identifiably different sorts, those open to justification, evidence, reasoning and argument, or in general those which have 'grounds'; and others which cannot be, or strictly *are* not, justified on grounds at all. The former division is relatively unproblematic and characterizes a range of statements or beliefs whose truth-values are determinable by standardly acceptable forms of argument. Observation, induction, deduction and hypothetico-deductive methods come into play here among procedures by which members of this group may be tested. They are sensitive to evidence and to validation by rational procedures, they can be known to be true or false. And here Wittgenstein asks a central question: how is it *possible* that a class of beliefs can have this distinctive feature of being open to rational justification?

What troubles him is the thought that although it is beyond question that we do provide justification and evidence for a vast bulk of judgments and that we are right to do so by the methods we standardly use, there is still a question about how a practice of this nature can be accounted for within our general conceptual scheme. It occurs to him that there can be no justified judgments unless some beliefs are ungrounded; if any beliefs are to be open to justification by appeals to evidence and argument then some beliefs must be accepted without them. The thesis of 'groundless belief' dominates Wittgenstein's discussion which is set initially in the epistemological context of the regress of justification; and it may seem, misleadingly as it turns out, to resemble foundationalism's search for a special terminus. It would be a mistake to see the point Wittgenstein wants to make as the proposal of an alternative regress-stopper. Reasons, he says, come to an end; and the question of where the end may be cannot be answered by invoking an epistemologically basic class of propositions. No terminus of *any* kind can explain certainty.

This uncompromising stand is a consequence of Wittgenstein's attempt to grapple with the total problem of justification by pushing beyond empiricism's limits to the actions of agents, and the constraints upon them, which make justification possible. Empiricism's weakness lies in a short-sighted strategy of explaining empirical certainty solely within algorithms of proof and accounting for knowledge by accounting only for the justification and truth of beliefs; questions about the convictions of believers and explanations of why they believe what they do, are left aside; reasons and evidence alone matter, and 'discovery' is invidiously separated from 'testing'. These very limitations result in a dilemma built into the structure of empiricist theory: either the grounds of certainty can be pushed back indefinitely, or grounds of an unconditional and terminal nature must be found. By being committed to a ceaseless search for 'grounds' empiricist theory is caught in a problem of its own making, Wittgenstein thinks, since its self-imposed limitations exclude just that area of human activity essential to any solution.

The class of 'groundless' beliefs forms an entrenched and heterogeneous group of an especially fundamental kind which people sharing a common background take as being firm beyond question. Wittgenstein accords them a privileged position in our life and practice, 'they form the foundation of all operating with thought'. Being 'empirical propositions which we affirm without special testing' they 'have a peculiar logical role in the system of our empirical propositions' and are 'the hinges' on which other beliefs turn.[2] As he frequently says, they are 'exempt from doubt' and their peculiarity is clear enough: they are empirical beliefs which are acknowledged in our practice to be unassailable.

Examples freely taken from the text bear this out unexceptionally: that the earth has existed for many years past, that motor cars do not grow out of the earth, that I have never been on the moon; that I have hands and a body with internal organs, that other people do; 'I believe that I have forbears, and that every human being has them. I believe that there are various cities, and, quite generally, in the main facts of geography and history. I believe that the earth is a body on whose surface we move and that it no more suddenly disappears or the like than any other solid body; this table, this house, this tree, etc.'[3] We are given a commonsense credo that draws upon Moore's examples of certain belief.

Two characteristics of these examples break decisively from foundationalist conceptions. They are vernacular expressions framed in realism's accessible language; and they are beliefs of widely different kinds, consisting of singular statements, generalizations, statements about other minds, the future or the past. That such a heterogeneous array of statements should be grouped together as standing in a fundamental relation to other statements appears puzzling if we make the mistake, which Wittgenstein warns against, of envisaging a foundation of knowledge fixed in the uniform grammar of first-person avowals. At certainty's source there is no common form of proposition; there is a class of mixed beliefs grouped together in terms of a common resistance to rejection.

Wittgenstein was impressed by the immovability of these beliefs, and he found especially striking the less obvious feature that their 'immovability' is not a result of their having been verified by evidence or validated by reasons. They are, in a sense, oblivious to evidence, if only because no evidence is more certain than the beliefs themselves. As he says, 'My not having been on the moon is as sure a thing for me as any grounds I could give for it.' Evidence and experiment may support a proposition's truth, yet 'whenever we test anything, we are already presupposing something not tested'. Do we then presuppose 'the truth of the proposition that the apparatus I believe I see is really there'? He answers that testing comes to an end, 'I do not doubt the existence of the apparatus before my eyes. I have plenty of doubts, but not *that*'; and 'the certainty here is the same as that of my never having been on the moon'.[4] Wittgenstein anticipates the reply that the 'groundless acceptance' of a belief's certainty must be, at any rate, an exceptional event unrelated to our ordinary practices. On the contrary, he says, 'regarding it as absolutely solid is part of our *method* of doubt and enquiry'; 'It belongs to the logic of our scientific investigations that certain things are *in deed* not doubted.'[5] If there is no appealing to evidence, the position of evidence is undercut; and if the truth or reason-ableness of these beliefs is a matter of their being justified on evidence, then they are neither true nor false, reasonable or unreasonable. Yet he insists that we are right to see them as being unassailable.

But why unassailable? One notable message from Quine is simply that 'unassailability' is out. The problem that drove Quine to this answer is put shrewdly by Wittgenstein's ques-tion, '*What* is to be tested by *what*? (who decides *what* stands fast?)'[6] According to Quine's second story there can be no definitive answer; like James, he thought all of a system's elements are plastic, the tug can go either way if the boundaries of inquiry enclose a structure where evidence facing evidence is pragmatically adjusted to organize experience. Wittgenstein wanted to preserve pragmatism's holistic insights without sacri-ficing the idea of entrenchment and he hits out at two targets at once: empiricism's restriction of epistemology to the distance to which justifying reasons can reach, and pragmatism's message that nothing can stand fast. Questions of *certainty* can-not be decided by using standing techniques of proof even though they are entirely appropriate to questions of justifica-tion and truth; instead, we must step outside them. He tells us that ungrounded beliefs 'lie apart from the route travelled by enquiry'.[7] Their unassailability is assured, but only if a move is made which neither Quine nor orthodox empiricists would accept. Epistemology must be shifted away from thoughts of a terminus in evidence and should focus on the explanation of entrenchment itself. So we find that the thrust of Wittgenstein's arguments in *On Certainty* is directed to the problem of accounting for the actions of ascribing agents in 'standing fast', as he says, with beliefs of the kind he has adumbrated. The departure from tradition is at its greatest here. We are moved back from foundations in grounded belief to the idea of ungrounded belief, and back further to action itself. Rejecting the idea of ultimate evidential grounds, he substitutes the idea of human action underpinning the certainty of beliefs. The view is expressed tersely: 'Giving grounds, however, justifying the evidence, comes to an end; – but the end is not certain propositions' striking us immediately as true, i.e. it is not a kind of *seeing* on our part; it is our *acting*, which lies at the bottom of the language game.' And he says, 'As if giving grounds did not come to an end sometime. But the end is not an ungrounded presupposition: it is an ungrounded way of acting.'[8]

Among the most important of Wittgenstein's contributions to general epistemology is his conception of the role of persons in the determination of empirical certainty. It challenges empiricist theory with a pragmatically inspired account of entrenchment in which resolute conviction expressed in the action of 'standing fast' with a belief can be firm base for certainty. But conviction itself must be explained, and extended passages of discussion take conviction back to its source in an interlocking network of beliefs, which he describes as one's 'picture of the world'. It strikes him that conviction presupposes the ability to connect a convincing belief with other beliefs within the network; a person is convinced to the point of certainty only because of the ways in which a given belief stands in relation to a system of other beliefs. The point is driven home with repeated force: 'What stands fast does so, not because it is intrinsically obvious or convincing; it is rather held fast by what lies around it'; 'It is not single axioms that strike me as obvious, it is a system in which consequences and premises give one another *mutual* support'; 'We are taught *judgements* and their connection with other judgements. *A totality* of judgements is made plausible to us'; 'What I hold fast to is not *one* proposition but a nest of propositions.'⁹ If we forget Quine's aim of assessing for truth, his remarks that beliefs are not tested singly but only in bunches comes near to the idea. Wittgenstein's sustained intention is to account for certainty by showing that nothing can be certain on its own, in isolation from a system of opinion. It is this very interlocking character of our beliefs, he thinks, which constrains us to 'stand fast' with some and not with others. And the reason is transparent; the doubting of a belief has consequences reverberating throughout one's world picture, 'If I wanted to doubt the existence of the earth long before my birth, I should have to doubt all sorts of things that stand fast for me'; 'There seem to be propositions that have the character of experiential propositions, but whose truth is for me unassailable. That is to say, if I assume that they are false, I must mistrust all my judgements.'¹⁰ The argument would have pleased James. It is a piece of classic pragmatism to reject a conjecture, such as the conjecture that 'without knowing it, perhaps in a state of unconsciousness, I was taken away from the earth', by reckoning that 'this would not fit into the rest of my convictions at all'.¹¹

If this is the strategy it is not altogether fresh news. And it is the strategy, up to a point; if consistency within a system of belief is to be upheld then there is a price to pay for the beliefs one has. To accept a belief is to accept its consequences however they may fall, and they may fall disruptively on our standing stock of opinions. In the case of groundless beliefs a person is constrained to believe, for example, that the earth has long existed, because the alternatives to it would radically disrupt the 'picture of the world' sustaining his aims, actions and ways of making sense of his experiences or his life. The alternative would be 'chaos'. Wittgenstein says that we *do* not doubt, and he repeatedly gives examples to show not only that we do not, but also *why* we do not: if he were contradicted on all sides about the name of an old friend 'then in that case the foundation of all judging would be taken away from me'; 'If Moore were to pronounce the opposite of those propositions which he declares certain, we should not just not share his opinion: we should regard him as demented'; 'I cannot depart from this judgement (that I have never been in Asia Minor) without toppling all other judgements with it'; 'It is quite sure that motor cars don't grow out of the earth. We feel that if someone could believe the contrary he could believe *everything* that we say is untrue, and could question everything that we hold to be sure.'[12] In these examples Wittgenstein revives the Jamesian disjunctive argument, 'Either I believe *this*, or I scrap the better part of my knowledge.' They supply reasons of an excellent sort explaining why a person does what he does, why he stands fast with certainty and why he cannot seriously doubt. Given a person's set of beliefs embedded in a cultural background, a doubt would be incomprehensible to him precisely because he grasps that it conflicts drastically with this background on which he does and must rely. The examples favour the pragmatist thought that the reconciliation of conflicts among beliefs is a matter of adjustment in the interests of preserving consistency and relieving strain. Yet Wittgenstein's strategy departs from James's pragmatism at a crucial point. James is trying to explain how beliefs are justified and how grounds can support their truth. Wittgenstein is not trying to do this, but trying to explain why people hold beliefs so tenaciously even if they are not able to give any reasons or bring forward any evidence in support of their certainty. The pressing matter for Wittgenstein at this stage is to demonstrate that some beliefs firmly held without evidence need not be held arbitrarily.

Avoiding the charge of arbitrariness was always an awkward matter for pragmatism. Consistency alone is neutral about choices, so direction must come from the end of achieving a coherent picture of experience. But pictures of experience can be as we make them and imagination is unconstrained, leaving

open the question of control. Wittgenstein's thesis of entrenchment is arguably a pragmatist variation, but it leaves James's
scheme behind in its attempt to explain rather than to justify
entrenched beliefs. James saw the process of pragmatic adjustment as a source of truth, albeit of a kind relating to current
experience and belief. Wittgenstein did not; truth-values are
assigned by an evidence-producing rationale, whereas certainty lies outside justification. In spite of this, on the strength
of deliberation of the kind James had in mind we can and do
stick firmly with beliefs. We hold them to be certain, not
because evidence establishes their truth, but because it is the
most rational action to take within the constraints of our
general scheme of belief. It is certainly true that beliefs like
'the earth has existed for many years' are not things we decide
about or choose to believe in the way we decide, say, whether
the Etruscans lived for many years. The former function as
'hinges' on which our other beliefs turn. But the fact that they
are woven into our cultural cloth or 'form of life' does not by
itself make them sacrosanct. They are unmovable because of
the *kind* of fit they have, involving a grasp of consequences,
and one which can be invoked, as Wittgenstein does, in
accounting for their unmovability by looking to an agent's
reasons for holding on to them in the absence of grounds. If a
person cannot give grounds for the certainty of the belief that
the earth has existed for many years (since the grounds he
might give are less certain than the belief they might support),
he is still in a position to say what would happen to the structure of his knowledge if he repudiated the belief. There is,
perhaps, a sense in which he has 'no choice' but to stick with
it; yet to say this is to mark the difference, not between his
having or not having a choice, but between a case in which
one has a choice between two equally rational though perhaps
not equally true alternatives, and the present case with its
alternatives of unintelligibility or the preservation of a view
that gives sense to the world. Given alternatives of this kind,
the action of sticking with the latter is backed by the best of

reasons there can be. The choice of entrenchment is pragmatically directed by the demands of intelligibility and adjustments to this end are necessarily rational adjustments, for the very idea of a 'rational adjustment' is tied to the selection of routes appropriate to one's ends. If a person aims at an intelligible view of the world, it is not an arbitrary matter to preserve it in the only way it can be preserved, and that way is to refuse the admission of beliefs whose acceptance would fatally impair it.

There are two dangers in shackling Wittgenstein in *On Certainty* with the exegetical view that education, training and experience within a larger 'form of life' are the final controls on our beliefs and practices, which become second nature with us by our participation in a culture; and that when we try to account for our beliefs, as in explaining certainty, the best we can say is something like 'Taking this as unquestionable is part of how we carry on.' First, this reading of *On Certainty* conveys that the buck stops, not with individuals responsible for their own actions and decisions within the constraints of a 'form of life', but with institutions distinctive of a culture. It still lives in the shadow of the sort of empiricism it tries to combat by perpetuating the model of external control, in this case ultimate control by social practices and cultural norms. Wittgenstein appreciated that we are held fast *within* an environment by our recognition of the effects which its constraints have on us, not held fast *by* an environment independent of our actions.

The second danger is that the interpretation stops the problem short of its solution in *On Certainty*. We may, fairly enough, describe the situation by saying that the context in which 'this is certain' is asserted does not make any room for the idea of a question's being asked. Although Wittgenstein considered this (or something close to it) to be right, he also saw that it is a bland answer – or an inadequate answer – to the question of *why* a practice is shaped in this way; and that any adequate answer will involve a person's awareness, acquired by training in a 'form of life', that questioning or doubting in such a case is perverse, crazy or as he often says 'unreasonable', and in turn that this awareness is bound up with a person's appreciation of what the consequences of questioning or doubting would have for himself. The major piece of argument from, roughly, 446 to 620 marks this development. It is significant that the argument does not maintain that the final determination of the certainty of a person's beliefs is a matter of whether they are embedded in his institutions or are with him second nature products of training. These things are, of course, central to the argument; yet a vexing question remains about the way in which these practices actually do constrain a person's beliefs. It is no answer simply to reaffirm the point that 'This is what we do', or to say that we hold beliefs to be certain because they are part of the 'form of life' in which we find ourselves. It is important that we can explain why we are closely bound to a 'form of life' and this cannot be done if 'one may say no more from within philosophy than, "Human life is like that"' and that 'Our task is a descriptive one.'[13] It seems that in *The Blue Book*, *Zettel* and partly in the *Investigations* (e.g. 217) Wittgenstein treated description as the goal; but in *On Certainty* the inadequacy of this answer goads him to push beyond it.

Like Quine and James, Wittgenstein warns against the consequences of rocking the boat too hard. Conservatism is the rule, for dissent from 'ungrounded' beliefs points away from intelligibility and towards the disintegration of a world view. To take his example, dissent from the belief that 'the water in the kettle on the gas flame will not freeze but boil' *could* be made intelligible, but only if causal factors sufficient to account for this failing to happen could be envisaged, and they would have to rest within a larger body of belief with minimal conflict. If this were to occur, Wittgenstein says, we would be astonished although still intelligibly integrated. We can adjust for novelty, he thinks, so long as our system survives the process. But the belief that the earth has existed for many years, and others of the kind, are different; the adjustments needed to accommodate dissent cannot be imagined without wrecking the system itself: 'Here a doubt would seem to drag everything with it and plunge it into chaos.'[14] The resources of our view of the world are incapable of providing for the possibility, and its boundaries limit the doubts we can rationally entertain. Wittgenstein's prominent remark, 'knowledge is in the end based on acknowledgment' is less puzzling than it may seem. Like James, he placed people at the centre, and it is up to individuals themselves to acknowledge and to be constrained by these boundaries. As he tells us, the acknowledgment is no more than the admission that 'There cannot be any doubts about it for me as a reasonable person.'[15]

Wittgenstein saw that if our *acting* lies at the bottom of the language-game then even the most deeply entrenched beliefs must be open to change. As he says, 'a language-game does change with time'.[16] Pragmatism's recipe for change takes its cue from Neurath's boat: any plank in a ship at sea can be replaced if others around it are used as a support. Wittgenstein's river bed analogy endorses Neurath's point that entrenched certainties are alterable; they are like the hardened banks of a river channelling the flow of less hardened opinions which, in turn, imperceptibly erode and alter the hard banks themselves. There is not a sharp boundary, he says, between the movement of the water and the shift of the bed. 'Would it be *unthinkable*,' he asks, 'that I should stay in the saddle however much the facts bucked?' The answer is no: 'Certain events might put me into a position in which I could not go on with the old language-game any further. In which I was torn away from the *sureness* of the game.'[17] That this could happen may appear as a puzzling undermining of certainty unless it is seen how essential this admission is to Wittgenstein's intention of locating the source of certainty in human action. One's actions of standing fast with beliefs are constrained by one's picture of the world and the picture itself might be modified. Whether a person *has* to be thrown out of the saddle depends upon his perception and assessment of the refractory events; he must be able to see what they come to and to grasp their impact on his own field of belief. And the impact, Wittgenstein insists, could be profound: 'We know that the earth is round' and 'We shall stick to this opinion unless our whole way of seeing nature changes.'[18]

So we find Wittgenstein moving towards a thesis in which believers hold firmly to beliefs, not because they have good reasons for asserting their truth, but because they have the best of reasons for their actions in refusing to reject them. He responds to the problem of how algorithms embodying the idea of evidentially supported belief are possible at all, with a unique answer. Although 'giving grounds' stops, rationally constrained action does not; it continues when individuals pragmatically take into account the consequences which the beliefs in question will have for their own lives. The Jamesian switch from pragmatism's operationalist mode of heeding the consequences of beliefs to its humanistic mode of heeding the consequences for the believers becomes, when ground-giving stops, Wittgenstein's guiding light.

It was certainly James's intention to discern a process that would generate truth-values for beliefs without putting the burden of control on immediate experience, and a holism liberally endowed with human interests seemed the best model. But it was, in its way, a poor choice; for there is no chance of conjuring truth from adjustments aimed at the preservation of consistency unless some beliefs contained in the system are indispensable to it. This would mean, James thought, the introduction of some sort of antecedent certainty independent of the pragmatic process, and it seemed to him a bad idea promoted by absolutist and rationalist theories. This slip in judgment was costly; the idea was bad only because James in common with his opponents saw 'certainty' as a kind of higher grade of universal truth validated by abstract reasoning or purified intuitions. Since these had no place in pragmatism, certainty had none either; and he was left with no real answer to the criticism that pragmatic processes give at best a degree of credibility, a position he also disliked. Whether Wittgenstein himself was aware of James's problem remains obscure although he had the answer to it; James's conception of the 'pragmatic mediation' of beliefs should be shifted away from the justification of true beliefs; 'certainty' is a consequence of pragmatic constraints on action, not of truth-determining argument.

Wittgenstein's breakaway from foundationalism is most striking in the idea that justification or proof, or in general a reliance on evidence and reasons, is funded by the actions of believers and that there is no *further* funding. He sketches a broad division between algorithms for justification and explanations of action; and, he thinks, any theory of testing is incomplete if either element of this division is neglected. Foundationalism's picture of certainty as springing from a 'kind of seeing' envisages the acquisition of certainty as an integrated part of procedures of justification; one appeals to intuitions, of an intellectualizing or a perceptual sort, as a truth-initiating evidential rung on the inferential ladder. The awkward part of the operation is not so much the construction of the ladder as the constitution of the rung at the bottom; to keep to the rules the rung has to carry its own certainty with it. In *On Certainty* Wittgenstein rejects this picture in favour of the idea that we can explain why a person 'stands fast' with a belief by looking to the constraints enforcing his action. And if there is no other explanation of certainty, as he insists, then 'explanations of certainty' stand apart from procedures of justification. They account for conviction without raising the question of evidence.

Surprisingly, perhaps, the idea has a Humean prototype. Hume's speculations about 'the operations of the mind which form the belief of any matter of fact' revealed a sensitivity to the importance of, to choose his words, 'the *manner* of conception' of empirical belief:

> I confess that it is impossible perfectly to explain this feeling or manner of conception ... Its true and proper name ... is *belief*,

which is a term that everyone sufficiently understands in common life. And in philosophy, we can go no farther than assert,
that *belief* is something felt by the mind, which distinguishes the
ideas of the judgement from the fictions of the imagination. It
gives them more weight and influence; makes them appear of
greater importance; enforces them in the mind; gives them a
superior influence on the passions, and renders them the governing principle of our actions.[19]

It is a pity that having got this far the flaws in Hume's
imagination-belief distinction should have concealed the advance these passages represent. In them Hume cuts through
the question of the validation of beliefs to the central issue of
the psychological constraints governing their acceptance and
establishes a precedent in empiricist epistemology for subordi-
nating the problem of justification to the Wittgensteinian problem of accounting for conviction. Hume saw no possible explanation, and it would be surprising if he could, given the
limitations of his reductive empiricism. Hume's neglected insight moves in the direction of Wittgenstein's richly developed
one with the lesson that the 'problem of justification' can be
solved only by first solving a problem about people and their
actions.

The idea invites a major epistemological shift from evidential roots to normative roots. The question 'Why stick with
this?' is a quasi-causal question having two sorts of answers,
'Because there is good evidence of its being so' and 'Because it
is incomprehensible for me to do anything else.' Wittgenstein saw that unless we can sometimes give the second answer
we can never give the first one. Surveying the totality of our
beliefs, there are many we justify on evidence and some we do
not; and we rely on the latter as fixed 'hinges' on which the
justifiability of the former turns, for example, we do not
question 'the existence of the apparatus' in testing, or that 'a
substance A always reacts to a substance B in the same way,
given the same circumstances', or that ...; and here there
is no systematic filling in of the blank, for the network of belief

does not *naturally* define an ordered sequence of statements. Each line of inquiry, pushed back in the light of our different interests, will turn up a miscellany of convictions pragmatically resistant to rejection. And this, Wittgenstein thinks, is an essential part of the 'system' within which 'all testing, all confirmation and disconfirmation of a hypothesis takes place'; without it there could be no such system and no conception of evidence or proof.

If we glance with hindsight at Quine it is fair to say, with that mixture of admiration and despair which Quine often engenders in his readers, how exceedingly close he came to combining the virtues of Wittgenstein and James in his radical reshaping of empiricism. The interesting question is why the distance between Quine and the James–Wittgenstein axis should be as great as it is. One reason is transparent. Quine retained in his revisionary view a crucial piece of theorizing belonging to logical empiricism, loosely summed up as an hostility towards the mind ill-disposing him to see conviction, however rationally held, as a source of certainty. His behaviourism kept him from looking beyond the assignment of truth-values. Yet he glimpsed with clarity that firmness approaching certainty was needed; according to his first story, observation sentences are 'nearly infallible' when keyed directly to present stimulations. Characteristically 'they are just the sentences on which a scientist will tend to fall back when pressed by doubting colleagues'.[20] The admission is significant and Wittgenstein would have challenged only the explanation that their firmness is due to closeness to stimulation and remoteness from theory. When uttered in straightforward contexts 'observation sentences' have a natural sense of rightness, one prior to philosophical theorizing and easily passed over. We fall back on them when pressed because of a second nature recognition of their resistance to rejection. Observations like 'This stuff is green' or 'The pointer points on the scale to 50 grammes' *could* be set aside as conflicting with more important beliefs; but largely there is no conflict and they are retained by a consciousness of the greater cost of expelling them. Mendacity apart, most of our face-to-data reports are restricted to assertions of experience whose rejection would have repercussions impossible to sustain, and it is understandable that empiricism should have singled them out as the ultimate vehicles of testing. But it is regrettable that their high resistance was credited to perceptual encounters with raw data. We can be pragmatically constrained to stick with 'This stuff looks green to me' as well as with 'I have never been on the moon', a reminder that the importance of perception lies less in a contribution to certainty than in its role of giving statements a contact with the observed world.

Moore sensed the pragmatic firmness of observation when he insisted that he *knows*, for instance, that he is seeing a tree in front of him despite his own doubts about *how* he knows. Wittgenstein's attitude is not altogether one of approval: 'Moore's mistake lies in this – countering the assertion that one cannot know that, by saying "I do know it." ' He thinks that Moore was right to be certain, to have no doubts whatever and to be as sure of it as he is of anything else. Although it struck Moore as proper to express his certainty in terms of his knowing, Wittgenstein balks at the idea. 'Whether I *know* something', he says 'depends upon whether the evidence backs me up or contradicts me'; knowledge calls for grounds and validating argument, ' "I know" relates to a possibility of demonstrating the truth.' Fundamental certainties like Moore's do not; they are groundless, and 'what we have here is a foundation for all my action. But it seems to me that it is wrongly expressed by the words "I know".' The argument is more than a piece of legislation and directly takes on the issue of the status of knowledge itself. 'Knowing' and 'being certain' are crucially different, he thinks: if certainty is guided by the pragmatic logic of conviction, 'the special logic of the concept "knowing" is not that of a psychological state'. Knowledge-claims invite justification, 'if he (Moore) knows something, then the question "How does he know?" must be capable of being answered', and 'if one does answer this question one must do so according to generally accepted axioms', those relating to standing ideas of evidence and inference.[21] So far, Wittgenstein's account of 'knowing' would fit easily within orthodox empiricism and he has no quarrel with the idea that knowledge-claims need rational backing by evidence. Just because of this, he insists, certainties like Moore's lie outside them. If knowledge presupposes the practice of supporting judgments by evidence or 'grounds', he argues, *this* activity in turn presupposes a different sort of practice in which we are pragmatically constrained to accept beliefs as certain without grounds. And if the certainties which Moore affirms are presuppositions of 'knowing', Moore cannot claim to know them without begging the question.

Wittgenstein's discussions have an importance beyond the domestic issue with Moore. They allow him to affirm pragmatism's traditional posture of fallibilism and undercut the opposition to it. By detaching knowledge from certainty he extends a pragmatic fallibilism over the range of claims subject to procedures of justification. The argument is concise: knowledge calls for grounds, and grounds can be overturned; but certainty does not call for grounds and can co-exist with fallibilism. Critics of fallibilism take their stand on the point that 'I know' implies 'I cannot be mistaken' and, like Moore, they ask too much of knowledge. Yet their intuitions about the limits of being mistaken are right: 'There are', Wittgenstein says, 'certain types of case in which I rightly say I cannot be making a mistake, and Moore has given a few examples of such cases.' The idea of 'being mistaken' relates a person to his view of the world just as 'being certain' does; one can be mistaken about a belief only if the possibility of its rejection can be intelligibly assimilated into one's scheme of things, only when 'a place is prepared in the game' for it; even if I could envisage how I might have got to the moon unawares, that *'would not give me any right* to speak of a possible mistake here. I play the game *wrong* if I do'.[22] The critics have crossed the

wrong wires and hooked up 'I cannot be mistaken' to knowledge instead of to certainty; and if hooked to the latter, fallibilism remains untouched with its message that knowledge is
no stronger than the grounds for it.

As a result of this manoeuvring, Wittgenstein enables pro-
ponents of fallible knowledge to defend themselves against the
criticism that all certainties have been scrapped. Peirce's defence of firmly true belief at the end of inquiry was an uneasy
concession to the criticism and James spotted one of its weak-
nesses: 'that ideal vanishing-point towards which we imagine
that all our temporary truths will someday converge' runs on
all fours with 'the perfectly wise man' and is no less divorced
from reality.[23] Equally telling is his suggestion that 'convergence' is a causal idea and since it has not yet occurred despite
a long history of opportunities the prospects for it are too slim
to justify any hopes. Yet James never glimpsed Wittgenstein's
diagnosis that a Peircean-type view, if not Peirce's own view,
is compromised by taking virtually certain truth to be a product of methods of testing. James's criticism is deservedly successful against the qualification 'in the long run'; but what
really matters, Wittgenstein thinks, is the erroneous funding of
'certainty' by justifying rationales, particularly those of scientific method, whether in the present or in the indefinite future.
James's oversight is understandable. The pragmatist conception of scientific method replaced empiricist and rationalist
methods of testing with holistic ones, convergence on final
truth had no chance at all in the new scheme, so the 'long run'
thesis was an easy victim of ridicule. But it was a major mistake
on James's part to restrict the usable notions of epistemology
to those fitting into a pragmatic system having the principal
aim of supporting beliefs and crediting truth-values. Despite
its advantages of casting a net over beliefs well outside science,
the result encouraged fallibilism at the expense of a type of
certainty which James's mediating system could not cope with.

The pay-off of placing the 'human contribution' at the
centre of control in an epistemology of evidence and justifica-

tion would be, James hoped, a profound shift away from empiricist or rationalist attitudes to a philosophy faithful to human institutions and practices as they actually are. But revolutions have a waywardness unforeseen by their authors and in James's case it was serious, as Wittgenstein's *On Certainty* message spells out: James's scheme invites a return to recycled versions of the old answers unless it is fundamentally overhauled. 'Certainty' is not open to *justification* by procedures of proof, whether of a pragmatic, foundationalist or of any other kind; it is open to *explanation* in terms of pragmatic reasoning of the kind James dwells on. James would have appreciated that in practice people will stick with some beliefs simply because they have to stick with them if their view of the world is to make sense. The thought is crudely expressed, but fastens on a vital point; an explanation of why people act as they do is an essential part of any epistemology sustaining a claim to account for knowledge. Epistemology cannot be restricted to the business of accounting for people's beliefs solely in terms of the reasons, evidence and grounds which validate them. This is perhaps the hardest medicine to take from Wittgenstein's prescription and applies to pragmatists and foundationalists alike. Wittgenstein saw that this restriction of scope leaves epistemology incomplete; there can be no algorithms of justification without a well-distributed ration of pragmatically constraining certainties expressed in people's actions.

CHAPTER 5

REASON AND PARTICULAR CASES:
JOHN WISDOM

What is it to 'respect the constraints of reason' as objectivity requires? The question by-passes the reply that ways of reasoning vary with the ways of the reasoners and that there are, or at least could be, ways of reasoning different from our own. This is a problem to be faced, but without urgency. For we have access only to our ways and it is not to be supposed that in *our* way of respecting reason's constraints nothing is to be learned about what we must share with others. So we should start on home ground first.

In moving to an answer we have the benefit of two centrally important insights. The first is Wittgenstein's conception of the normative base of epistemology; in the end it is what people *do* that matters and what they do is open to rational explanation, an explanation which may be different from any explanation of why their beliefs are true or justified. The second is John Wisdom's conception of the fundamentals of rational thinking expressed in his remark that 'at the bar of reason always the final appeal is to cases'. In the end it is what people do in *particular cases* that matters, and what they do is move from case to case by their own lights.

It was the empiricists' intention to roll back the constituents of reasoning until the bare elements lay exposed. Their vision was endowed with an adaptable fund of theory and marked by a determination, of a particularly unrelenting kind in Hume, to discern the primary grounds of reasoned belief, if such grounds there were. The upgrading of Hume by logical analysis gave incisiveness to the tradition and a canonical answer to the problem of what the constraints of reason must be by dividing the scope of justification between the operations of observation and logic. This refreshed thesis seemed a simple and portable framework capable of assaulting old problems at the roots of theory. It was not to last, yet the relegation of the thesis to the basket of naive theories neglected its deep psychological impact. It is one thing to reject programmatic reductionism or the verification theory of meaning, but another, and as some saw it a quite impossible thing, to repudiate the thought that argument rationally constrains only through logical or inductive success. What else, indeed, could there be?

The question 'When does an argument constrain a person's judgments with the force of reason?' is centrally positioned in Wisdom's later philosophy. It is a question about the primary constraints on a person's freedom to draw conclusions from evidence, and Wisdom addresses himself to the job of discrediting positivist-inspired restrictions on the scope of reason. Principles, rules and premises can function as they do, he argues, only if they are logically subservient to the particular instances to which they refer. He is impressed by the fact that one cannot understand rational justification in its final stages unless one understands the role of particular cases in reasoning. And his intention is to cut us loose from the idea that the justification of a judgment, *any* judgment, must in the end appeal either to general premises or to direct observation.

Why should it be, as Wisdom thinks, that the primary ground upon which we decide whether a particular case is one of a certain sort can never be a premise, rule or definition giving the general identifying criteria of things of that sort? It might be argued that if any concept is to be bound by premises, rules or definitions, some concepts must not be if a regress is to be avoided. The argument is cogent but does less than justice to the epistemological precedence which, in Wisdom's view, must be accorded to particulars. If, Wisdom asks, general criteria of identity are to remain open to the possibility of refutation by contrary particular cases, how can the criteria act as a final court of appeal? Since they must give way to counter-instances to avoid dogmatism, clearly they cannot. The final appeal must be, instead, to cases themselves.

This answer seems unconvincing. If the power lies with the particular cases, what gives a case its power to overrule criteria? Not, in theory, appeal to further criteria. Nor can a defensive decision rule out the possibility of counter-instances short of a plunge to conventionalism; and anything less than this leaves the authority of identifying criteria weaker than the authority of the refuting cases. So if criteria of identification depend on the unaided identification of particulars, a person must in some sense know that a counter-example *is* a counter-example without drawing on general criteria. But how can one know? If Wisdom is right and appeals to general criteria of identification – premises, definitions, rules – cease to exercise final control, the alternatives of intuitionism, subjectivism or just plain ascriptive anarchy loom convincingly. The policy of scrapping Humean-type restrictions seems a foolhardy concession.

Yet it was a policy which James and Kuhn followed. For James, Clifford's Hume-like strictures simply did not accord with any conception of reasoning that was both real and usable; they excluded too much, were too procrustean and disclosed a philosophical insularity from the world of actual practice. That Kuhn would agree is evident in his sharp rejection of the idea that theory-choice decisions are determined by logic and observation alone. If such choices find a close analogue in value-decisions without back-tracking on rationality, as he thinks, then the traditional dichotomy is undercut. The trouble was that their shared thesis clashed with entrenched 'Humean' presuppositions. If Kuhn was more alive to this than James, neither philosopher mounted a successful attack on the opposition's fundamental ideas, and unless this could be persuasively pulled off there was little chance of shifting opinion. Hence the

value of Wisdom's unique analysis; for it is directed less to
issues in the philosophy of science, or in James's case the problems of truth, freedom and the external world, than to what
Wisdom calls the 'ultimate logic' of justification. The target is
just that body of primary philosophical theory blocking the
advance.

Wisdom agrees that both inductive and deductive methods
of argument rationally constrain. At issue is their epistemological status and the question of whether they exhaust the scope
of reason. He argues unequivocally that they do not; neither
form of reasoning is epistemologically fundamental and we
must push back further.

Induction is a clear case in point. Since induction justifies
conclusions by pointing to regularities, prior to inductive
generalizing it must be decided whether to regard an array of
instances as being instances of similar or of different sorts. But
regularity presupposes similarity and the perception of differences, so decisions about whether a given number of cases
constitute a regular sequence, on the basis of which we might
predict, cannot themselves be justified inductively. Fundamentals remain still untapped.

In the case of deductive inference we must push back in two
dimensions, Wisdom thinks. First, deduction's transmission of
truth on fixed rails of inference ensures that every reason for
or against the conclusion of a valid argument is also and
equally a reason for or against the premises, so the fact that a
conclusion follows by deduction from the premises cannot be
an ultimate ground for asserting or denying the conclusion.

Second, when we push back the claim that the conclusion
follows by deduction from the premises, the claim itself emerges
as being parasitic on reasoning of a non-deductive kind. We
standardly test the validity of an argument by an inspection
procedure to determine whether it has the same form as some
valid argument; thus we take an argument to be valid if it is
a substitution instance, or reducible to a substitution instance,
of a logical truth. And, as Wisdom points out, the thesis that

an argument is valid when it is an instance of some valid form is not itself formally valid or a rule of any logical system, but expresses a practice underwritten by non-demonstrative inference from parallel cases. For example, given a valid sentence built only of logical particles and blanks 'Every F that is G is F' one consequently assents to, or is in some sense constrained to assent to, the validity of the sentence 'Every man who is bald is a man.' But if we push back and ask *why* one is constrained, the answer is not that one is constrained by valid inference but by the comparability or parity of the sentences. One sees them as like each other, as subjects for the same symbolic generalization. We test validity by inspection as a final check on our formulas; and inspection is no more than inspection for parity in relevant respects, that is, parity by our lights. It seems to follow that the ascription of validity, thus pushed back, is ultimately non-deductive and rests on the discernment of parallel cases, or as Kuhn would say, on the assimilation of similar exemplars without answering the question, similar in respect of what?

Successful results in a formal proof depend on the conviction that the axioms are logically valid and that the rules of inference never lead from truth to falsehood, hence a problem about how to cash 'conviction' whether we choose semantic or syntactic standards. One might fall back on self-evidence or intuition although they explain little by themselves. Wisdom quarrels less with them than with the idea that to invoke these labels is to fall back on self-evident principles and rules. To be 'self-evident' is simply to be evident to a person, without aid from elsewhere, that something is beyond denial; and self-evidence like 'intuition' reveals the dependence of the discernment of validity on the perceptiveness of agents. Suppose that we demonstrate a particular argument's validity by appealing to the semantic principle that 'any argument is deductively valid if it is impossible that the premises should be true and the conclusion false', and let self-evidence be the defence of the principle. In turn 'self-evidence' is defended by the production of immediately recognizable particular logical truths; there is a switch from logic to ostentation, for we aim at luminosity and that depends on contingent ability. We choose instances differing from the one to be proved by the principle only in respect of exemplary simplicity and we allow conviction to rest on the perception of parity. So why not exchange 'self-evidence' for the perception of parity and difference, and join Kuhn in claiming that knowledge of fundamental ideas is embodied in the perception of similar cases prior to codification in principles? Any attempt to prove a conclusion C from premises P is valid only when every comparison required for the establishment of C is also required for the establishment of P, as Wisdom says. So there is no reason in theory not to set aside the principle and tackle contingent frailty by directly comparing the case to be proved by the principle with simple, and so on to recondite, examples from the range of cases in terms of which the principle is defended. The procedure is not formally valid; but this is a virtue, for no formally valid procedure can ultimately guarantee the formal validity of an argument.

Yet the thought keeps returning that mere parity hardly captures the concept of conclusive argument as we have it. True enough, parity is essential in areas of reasoning where conclusiveness matters most. Tests for consistency rest on parity no less than do tests for validity. Nevertheless the idea of conclusiveness still seems embedded in the idea of deductive inference, essential though parity may be.

Wisdom attempts to undermine this belief by the thesis that a deductive proof of any conclusion is no stronger or more conclusive than an argument which dispenses with general premises and appeals directly to similarities and differences between particular cases. He envisages justification in its final form as a procedure of argument in which a person gives or acquires reasons for ascribing a predicate to a particular case by comparing that case with other cases to which the predicate applies, and with still others to which it does not. Reasoning, when pushed to its limits, is reasoning by parallel cases.[1] And this is so even in logic; the deduction of a conclusion from a premise, Wisdom says, 'comes to no more than a case-by-case proof of that conclusion'. They are alternatives differing in form and convenience but not in conclusiveness. When rules occur they do so only inessentially; the difference between proof by deduction and proof by parallels is a difference in style with evidence and conclusion remaining the same, and rules drop out when the style is shifted. If a person argues 'This has twelve edges, for it is a cube and every cube has twelve edges' he is open to the criticism that the argument is circular if the general premise includes the case in question or invalid if it does not. What this criticism reveals, Wisdom thinks, is not a weakness in deduction but an appreciation of its real function and an explanation of its strength. To argue in this deductive way is to do no more than to bring to bear on the particular case at issue all the possible particular cases which support the principle mentioned except the case at issue; and these are cases which could have been brought to bear directly by arguing case-by-case.

Wisdom's critique of deduction is not an attack on deductive reasoning but a reappraisal of its epistemological position. The tradition he opposes had been questioned independently of his own views, for deduction's justification is less secure than may appear. An inductive justification of valid inference is insufficiently strong, for it can establish at best that valid arguments are usually though not always truth-preserving. On the other hand, a deductive justification of valid inference is necessarily circular.[2] If there is to be a justification of deductive inference at all it must lie outside both types of inference. But specifically where? It might be argued that appeal can be directed to an argument schema such as *modus ponens*, thus returning to the idea that parity of form with a valid form guarantees validity. And this seems to support Wisdom's thesis, although there is a serious snag. What, in this view, could justify the schema itself?

A direct appeal to instances may seem too much like induction to be a genuinely independent option. And it might be thought that Wisdom's procedure, like Mill's, is flawed for this reason. Despite the clear debt to Mill, Wisdom's analysis repays the debt by a revision of Mill's view on just this point. Mill argued that deductive arguments are, theoretically at least, eliminable in favour of direct non-deductive inference from singular instances comprising the evidence for the general statement itself. The results of deductive reasoning can be obtained with equal certainty, though not with equal convenience, by dispensing with general statements and reasoning directly from particulars to particulars.[3] So much of Mill's view Wisdom accepts. He differs from Mill in refusing to restrict the scope of 'argument from particulars to particulars' to inductive inference. The justifying grounds of a generalization, which Mill took to be the contingent evidence of similar instances actually observed, in Wisdom's thesis consist of instances which may be actual or possible indifferently and which form a general statement's extension; there is no existential restriction on particular cases evidentially admissible, as there is in Mill; it is enough that they should be conceivable cases.

More serious is the criticism that an argument from instances, as Susan Haack says, 'shifts the justification problem from the argument schema to its instances, without providing any solution to the problem of the justification of the instances, beyond the bald assertion that they *are* justified'.[4] Argument from parallels between cases seems at most to justify the transmission of a verdict from one case to another, without justifying the verdict itself in any given case; it may pass the buck but never bring it to rest. If this is so, the door to anarchy opens once again. The trouble with deduction is that it can transmit but not initiate truth, and this also seems to be the trouble with reasoning by parallels. The threat of Achilles hangs over them both.

Yet the threat can be met and Wisdom can call on Kuhn as a strong ally. It strikes Wisdom and Kuhn that what can be called 'learning what the instances of a sort of thing are' is just learning to see different cases as comparable in the way ascribers sharing the same background see them. And it seems that, if speakers share the same language, this background of practice must be rich enough for ascription to be restrained by a common understanding and concurrence in grasp of the subjects of reference acquired through education, training and experience. For it is only by acquiring a shared ascriptive tradition that individuals are able to describe the world in the same way, and they must come to the business of justifying their ascriptions forearmed with this common understanding. A procedure like Wisdom's establishes the comparability of instances in question to those belonging to this common background by fitting cases under test into a shared and, in Wittgenstein's sense, 'inherited' context. Reasoning by parallels *has* to have the capacity to justify ascription since it reveals whether or not fresh cases are comparable to the range of cases to which reference must be made if a predicate is to be understood. By establishing the connections of affinity and difference between a case at issue and a totality of possible cases encompassing a concept's extension, one appeals to the roots of reference where learning begins.

The interlocking elements of Wisdom's strategy now come together. If the justification of a judgment cannot rest on an appeal to general premises or criteria, he thinks, it cannot rest on direct observation either: the answer to a question of fact is not given with given data. Throughout his discussion Wisdom opposes the thesis that once all the data are in, once there is no question of 'looking and listening further', any remaining question about the data ceases to be a real, factual question and becomes one of words, attitude or persuasion. He remarks that undoubtedly a factual question can be predictive or 'speculative', for example, when a person speculates that a fox is in the tall grass from seeing only a head, he ventures a prediction about what may or may not be confirmed by further observation. On the other hand, a question about an actual state of affairs may survive observation and not be a speculative matter but a reflective one:

> For instance why not take the case of an accountant who has before him the assets and liabilities of a firm and asks 'Are they solvent?' or a statistician who has before him the records of births and deaths for the last 50 years and asks 'Has the average man today a greater expectation of life than he had 20 years ago?'[5]

The importance of these cases does not lie in the point that they are clear counter-examples to the general thesis that questions of fact must call for further observation. Wisdom is hunting bigger game and chooses these examples of *deductive* reflection deliberately as ones which his opponents are bound to accept:

> Here are questions which can be settled on the basis of facts already ascertained and which are yet definite questions which can be settled by an agreed, definite mathematical, deductive procedure.
>
> We all know and, what is more, we all recognize that there are questions which though they don't call for further investigation but only for reflection are yet perfectly respectable because the reflection they call for may be carried out in a definite demonstrative procedure which gives results Yes or No. My point is that this isn't the only sort of reflection and that the other sorts are not poor relations.[6]

The argument is something of a triumph. We must, and do in practice, allow that cases of the deduction of a conclusion from premises describing the data can be legitimate examples of the reflective settlement of factual issues; and if the deduction of a conclusion from premises comes in the end to no more than, is no more certain than, a procedure of the comparison of instances case-by-case, we are bound to allow that reflection by the comparison of cases is *equally* legitimate in the settlement of factual questions. By this deft move 'Humean' constraints on the scope of reason have been thrown off. There is no philosophical mistake in giving reasons by the perceptive comparison of instances which are, as Wisdom says, 'like the legs of a chair, not the links of a chain'. The avenues of rational argument closed by Humean theorizing at once become open for use.

It is precisely at this point that Wisdom's critics lose patience. What Wisdom has offered, it will be argued, is an intuitive process. Parallels between cases are parallels as a person sees them and others with different backgrounds, aims and values may see them differently. Since we are left, as Kuhn admits, 'with the absence of criteria able to dictate the choice of each individual', what passes for reasoning is really persuasion and psychology has elbowed out logic. 'Reasons' in Wisdom's sense are subjective and soft; we are no better off than with the 'reasons' of Kuhn and James.

Before bowing to the criticism we should look to its multiple origins and first note that it is rooted in the idea that validating reasons must be impersonal. James had hard words about this and his arguments strike home. Yet the desire for impersonalized reason is linked with the desire for general criteria and can be a transparent reminder that in validating reasons there is something universal which one ascriber must share with another. 'Impersonalized' reason must fail to connect persons, yet the call for it points to what does matter, the need for some common ground.

Second, the criticism is rooted in the Problem of Achilles.[7] Like Wisdom's 'reasoning by cases' the problem appears as a blot on the rational landscape: any demonstration generates an indefinite regress of premises, so no demonstration can be demonstratively justified. We may see Achilles as 'the problem of securing a secure premise' and look to our intuitions, or as 'the problem of turning premises into rules of inference' and short-circuit the regress. But intuitions are unexplanatory and the idea that premises under the label of 'rules' can stand back independently while controlling inference is implausible. Thus viewed, the puzzle stands; but there is another perspective. We can see Achilles not as a problem but as the lesson that it is *false* that in the absence of rules decisions are unjustified. Achilles's sound point that decisions about rules cannot finally rest on rules echoes Kuhn's sound point that the question 'Similar in respect of what?' does not always apply. And it is compatible with Wisdom's sound point that in reasoning by cases we prove the truth of a particular case by proving its comparability to the cases presupposed in any attempt to demonstrate its truth.

Third, rationality seems at risk. Few, least of all Wisdom, would query the idea that where there are incompatible ascriptions to a particular case, only one at most can apply; and it is probably the belief that this idea will be at risk unless criteria of the required generality can be found, which makes the view that they are needed so compelling. Yet the risk is illusory. What matters for rationality is not whether this or that feature of similarity or difference is the right or the relevant feature, but whether there is concurrence in the idea that features of similarity and difference *however they may fall* really matter, and matter enough to act as a brake, restriction or constraint on what one infers or concludes. It is undisputed that decisions about points of comparability are important in reasoning, but they are important only because a prior importance is accorded to this fundamental thought. Unless this were so, the notion that a person can be brought to change his mind about his judgment by showing that a case he accepts is comparable to a different case which he rejects would have no place in our, or in any, scheme of thinking. For there would be no notion of a reason committing or compelling a person to a judgment and so no conception of accepting or rejecting a judgment on the basis of evidence.

Fourth, the criticism looks for reasons and not for comparisons. Here it forgets what it well knows. To recognize a particular case as being an identifiable case of a certain identifiable sort, a person must see it as the same subject of a prior or subsequent identification, and as the same kind of subject as other identifiable cases. Neither condition will hold unless the particulars in question are seen as comparable instances; and to identify a particular case as being 'the same thing' as the same case encountered on other identifying occasions, and as being 'the same kind of thing' as comparable particular cases encountered elsewhere, is to take similarities and differences between cases to be *reasons* among others, for one's verdict.

Moreover, inferences to singular conclusions from general premises, or to general conclusions from sets of singular premises, could not be possible unless it were also possible to qualify arrays of particular cases in terms of general sortal statements; and this could not happen unless similarities and differences between individual cases were decisive constraints on grouping them into sorts. This much is undisputed, but it does not explain *why* parallels between cases should constrain a person to place them together as bearers of a common general predicate; it must also be understood, even if unvoiced, that by pointing to parallels one is pointing to reasons for doing what one does. To secure rational discussion at all it is necessary to allow that a judgment in one case commits a person to a similar view in comparable cases; and that, if a judgment in a particular case is true, dissent from it will be mistaken in any parallel case. To allow this, as we do in rational moments, is to acknowledge that comparisons between cases can be *reasons* constraining how one judges. To look for reasons is, often, *just* to look for comparisons.

Fifth, the criticism is rooted in the belief that the comparison of cases lacks discipline and can impose no rational control on the conclusions which people may reach. Since general criteria can aim at commensurability by ironing out individual differences between individual claims, can they be set aside even in theory? An answer must relieve the philosophical tension between the idea that decisions should rest with people and the idea that decisions should be rational, for it seems that idiosyncratic judgment shakes rationality by shaking commensurability. And tensions there are, coming from three strong options. On the one hand the thought that ascriptive decisions must in the end be up to individuals points persuasively to subjectivism. On the other, it is convincing to think that individual decisions must be responsive to some shared background, culture or identifiable 'form of life' and this thought points persuasively to relativism.

The third option is the view of Wisdom's critics and starts with the premise that there is no justified ascription in the absence of general criteria, standards or principles. They argue that shared judgments require shared criteria, so some standards must be common to all rational men, otherwise the pointers to subjectivism or relativism would be right. Because the subjectivist and the relativist assent to the critics' premise even if they object to the conclusion, the three options are linked. The subjectivist argues that each individual has his own standards of judgment while the relativist argues that standards are related to each community, culture or framework. The subjectivist judges by his own lights, the relativist by communal lights and both owe an allegiance to their respective principles.

Wisdom had the insight to see that, although the critics' premise is false, if there is genuine disagreement at the most fundamental level of reasoning, there has to be some common ground. Commensurability is indispensable although it appears in unexpected ways. In a dispute about parallel cases ascribers of predicates necessarily share standards of rational control, for if they argue to opposing conclusions by arguing about whether parallels do or do not hold between cases, they cannot argue about whether parallels matter. It follows at once that they cannot contest the idea that similarities and differences between cases are reasons for judging as they do. It is just because they have this in common that each refuses to accept the conclusion of the other. Each accepts something the other accepts, that some affinities and differences would be decisive, so each is subject to a rational constraint to which the other is subject. Since they dispute *which* affinities and differences are decisive they genuinely disagree. Since they share the idea that parity of cases rationally demands sameness of ascription they share a common rationality. Commensurability is preserved by the actions and discussions of individuals concurring in the idea that comparabilities and differences between cases must constrain judgment.

Hence the critics make no mistake in looking for common ground. The mistake is to look for it in the wrong place under the guidance of the false premise shared with the subjectivist and the relativist. And this is the premise which Wisdom denies with the support of Kuhn and the sympathy of James. Wisdom forces us to recognize that if anything must be common to different persons engaged in rational debate it has to be accepted by each of them on occasions when they disagree about the application of a term to a particular case, or disagree about standards of relevance appropriate to cases of the kind in question. We must reject the idea that the common ground between them can be a possible subject for dispute, without rejecting the idea that there is common ground. So we must reject the belief that the common ground consists of general individuating criteria or standards of relevance since they are, or can be, themselves subjects of dispute.

The thought here leads back to Wittgenstein's theme that actions take over when reasons stop. If Wisdom is right, our issues are discussable only if some of our actions are not; we cannot rationally debate whether parity constrains since the very idea of rational debate presupposes that it does. He saw that what matters is not the propositional content of beliefs or principles, which does indeed shift under revisionary pressure, but a common way of acting which makes revision possible. Behind reasoning lies a commitment to respect the constraints of parity, a form of action which competing views must have in common if issues are to be objectively discussible. Like Wittgenstein's 'groundless beliefs' the constraints of comparison are indispensable in getting an intelligible purchase on the world.

Wisdom's critique may still seem unsatisfying. It tells us that to respect the constraints of reason is in the last analysis to respect the constraints of the comparison of instances, so it does not satisfy the philosophical demand for a decision procedure for settling issues decisively. The appeal to individuating criteria is, or is part of, one such procedure. But as Wisdom remarks, it is better to face the fact that we do not have foolproof rules than to pretend that we have, especially since they are not needed. And facts like this one are hard to face, for decisive procedures of decision permit a subtle evasion of choice, one welcome enough to account for our psychological reluctance to abandon them. 'The more definite the instructions', Wisdom says, 'the less the anxiety for our own responsibility';[8] and it is a natural, perhaps a distinctively human trait to be dissatisfied with, to disown or even to fear a sort of reasoning which thrusts responsibility for judgment directly upon oneself.

CHAPTER 6

RATIONALITY, RELATIVISM AND OBJECTIVENESS

The route to objectivity has been historically marked by a search for some common ground guaranteeing interpersonal discussion and the settlement of differences. That an explanation of objectivity must pick out this common ground is implicit in the thesis that it is to be found in a world of external realities, but the postulation of common ground outside offered an impersonal basis and failed to be explanatory. The alternative of looking favourably towards agreement or consensus as the fabric of objectiveness opens the gates to conventionalism as an explanation of the fact of consensus itself; it makes access to objectivity dependent upon the things we consensually believe, trapping objectivity in the bias of agreed wisdom. Perhaps the trouble lies in the assumption that there *is* something to be shared, and the answer is to be found in the radical thought that there is no common ground at all. Once we admit that ways of reasoning vary with the ways of the reasoners, the scope for common ground seems too narrow to escape relativism, and the admission marks the fact that there are different institutions, different practices and different styles in approaching the world. Tolerance we may have, but no claim to universality for our own ways.

Wittgenstein was exercised by this thought and knew that his own views were likely to be seen as steering to relativism. The suggestion is there in the idea that one can 'stand fast' only within a context or 'nest' of beliefs giving sense and purpose to one's hold on the world; if there is one nest, there may be others not all the same, and if a bridge between them is needed it has to be found. Wittgenstein imagines people who share a form of life different from our own, they do not regard as telling reasons those which we take as good grounds in our system of belief; they ignore the propositions of physics and are guided by oracles. 'If we call this "wrong", he asks, 'aren't we using our language-game as a base from which to *combat* theirs?' And he replies, 'I said I would "combat" the other man – but wouldn't I give him *reasons*? Certainly; but how far do they go? At the end of reasons comes *persuasion*. (Think of what happens when missionaries convert natives.)'[1]

Wittgenstein's unorthodox attitude to the problem of relativism shares relativism's premise that one's reasons reach no further than the limits of one's picture of the world. Yet he counters the relativist conclusion that the system-dependency of reasoning prevents rational discussion across radically different cultures. Reasoning is logically bound to a background, he thinks, but the barriers to understanding other backgrounds are contingent. The effect of his argument removes relativism's sceptical bite. Here it is necessary to see that by 'persuasion' Wittgenstein means something like *instruction*: if a person thinks that the earth originated 50 years ago 'We might instruct him: The earth has long ... etc. – we should be trying to give him our picture of the world. This would happen through a kind of *persuasion*.' He repeatedly returns to the idea:

> Men have believed that they could make rain; why should not a king be brought up in the belief that the world began with him? And if Moore and the king were to meet and discuss, could Moore really prove his belief to be the right one? I do not say that Moore could not convert the king to his view, but it would be a conversion of a special kind; the king would be brought to look at the world in a different way.
>
> The existence of the earth is rather part of the whole *picture* which forms the starting-point of belief for me.
>
> If someone asked us 'but is that *true*?' we might say 'yes' to

him; and if he demanded grounds we might say 'I can't give you any
grounds, but if you learn more you too will think the same.'

If a child asked me whether the earth was already there before
my birth, I should answer him that the earth did not begin only
with my birth, but that it existed long, long before.... In
answering the question I should have to be imparting a picture
of the world to the person who asked it.[2]

These passages emphasize Wittgenstein's pragmatic point
that beliefs cannot be justified or grounded in isolation from a
fabric of other beliefs constituting a 'picture of the world'.
There is no discussing truth-values or the evidence for them in
the absence of an appreciation of the background within which
they are embedded, and psychological shifts must often
precede a willingness to consider and act on beliefs which have
no appeal to one's nature. Reasons impress only if they weigh
with a person enough to make him responsive to certain lines
of thought and action making sense to him against the attitudes and beliefs which, as James says, he 'has in stock'. Wittgenstein saw that this point applies not only within our own
culture, where the absorption of a 'picture of the world' is a
prerequisite for rational discussion among its members, but
also across alien cultures where the absorption of their fabric
of beliefs is a condition of discussions with them. If the practice
of relying on reasoning, evidence and proof cannot occur independently of 'the environment within which arguments have
their life', then giving our reasons to people who lack our
environment will be of no use. They must first be instructed in
the rudiments of our ways of doing things, forgetting for a
while about evidence. And here Wittgenstein hits on the term
'persuasion' to express an activity in which a scheme of things
is conveyed to someone with the intention of convincing without justifying; it is a preparation for believing on the strength
of evidence.

Wittgenstein's strategy sifts the good from the bad in relativism. The relativist's good idea that reasons and beliefs are
tied to reasoners and believers and their backgrounds can be

retained while rejecting the bad idea that system-dependency is a necessary barrier to rational discussions across cultures. Beliefs and backgrounds form a single package and, with effort and patience, the package is accessible.

Yet this is not the whole story. A relativist will argue that the beliefs involved have no more than local credibility. And this, relativism assumes, is as far as we can go: to bridge frameworks by instruction is not to test them against a common standard, and without common standards 'objective' becomes 'objective for us'. The problem of relativism reduces to the problem of what one person must share with others, any others, if the constraints of reason are to be respected.

Rationalism offers a global solution to the problem. There must be a shared core of belief in the form of universal assent across the cultural board to the truth of some proposition or propositions, judgments, concepts or rules. The solution quickly runs into trouble, for it seems indefensible in the face of the relativist reply that there is no common ground since there is no evidence of a contingent kind to support a thesis of universal belief. The rationalist route of argument is plausible only if it is transcendental. The conflict discloses that both the rationalist and the relativist accept the premise that *if* there are no universal beliefs, then there is no common ground. But should they accept it? Rationalism's transcendental appeal must stay with the truistic result that there has to be *something* which reasoners share if they are to be reasoners at all, for it risks refutation by implying universal belief. It puts a case for commensurability rather than for universal agreement, so there is no need to strain credibility by posits conflicting with how the world is. Because the relativist is right in affirming the antecedent that there are no universal beliefs, and the rationalist is right in denying the consequent that there is no common ground, neither of them should accept the premise. Since each is right in his own way, reconciliation seems possible if the premise is repudiated. The relativist can no longer oppose objectivity by arguing that there is no common ground because there are no universal beliefs, and the rationalist cannot defend objectivity by arguing that there is common ground because there are universal beliefs. Both bad arguments disappear, and with them the conflict between the views. Yet their surviving joint commitment to the idea that unless there is common ground there is no objectivity remains an issue. If the elusive 'common ground' cannot be universally shared belief, what can it be like?

Objectivity has the important property of spanning disagreement. It can apply on occasions when there is agreement or when there is dispute, or when one's evidence establishes one's case and when it does not. The winner and the loser of a debate can be equally objective in their assumptions, arguments and verdicts, and true judgments can be made with the same objectivity as false ones. In a certain sense objectivity has a bivalent neutrality, and it is largely this which gives us a respect for those with whom we disagree. It is surprising that premises recording disagreement between persons or cultures should often be taken as evidence of the absence of objectivity when it is plain that the two notions are mutually consistent. The mistake is likely to be made if objectivity is tied too closely to the idea of agreement, inviting the question 'Agreement about what?' and relativism's answer that 'agreement' does not go beyond the limits of local beliefs. But a respect for people's actions does. One of the by-products of Wittgenstein's hugely important insight that action is at the bottom of knowledge is simply that we are not forced to take beliefs, criteria, rules, or some conjured-up propositional content as the topic of agreement; equally it does not force us to the idea that there is *nothing* universal in objectiveness. What objective ascribers must share is a form of action evinced in the 'common behaviour of mankind' which enables men to view the world by the different lights which guide them.

In *our* styles of thinking the constraints of rationality guide our actions as objective agents and show themselves in a variegated way. At one end of the objectivity spectrum we acknowledge standards of inductive strength and deductive validity, value consistency and the force of evidence, and follow argument where it leads even if against our interests. All in an ideal world, no doubt, and it is often an ideal more or less maintained in the maintenance of one's objectiveness. Yet it is not the only one, since rationality is responsive to the practical as well as to the academic virtues; objectivity can appear in a preparedness to stand back and view evidence impartially against patterns of conflicting human differences without a self-conscious allegiance to formal canons of argument. Like any virtue, objective behaviour is a disposition with its own demands which agents must be prone to meet if they are to lay claim to it. Yet it is fair to say that even if these variable demands are, or should be, valued by *us*, they are hardly a light which guides everyone else. As a relativist sees it, the span of our own forms of rationality is not the important point; what matters most is that the package of practices belonging to our institutions is not, or does not have to be, respected universally. And the rationalist is troubled by this relativist intervention, all the more for its being true. His response is to push back to necessities beyond the relativist's contingent facts and insist that 'there has to be an epistemological unity of mankind' as a condition of discourse at all.[3] Admittedly the case in favour of unity is inauspiciously thin since the claim seems empty of specifiable content. Even the laws of logic are just more grist to the relativist's mill. The rationalist is in the predicament of having insight without evidence, and evidence is rightly needed. But where to look for it? Our own inductive and deductive styles of argument remain open to relativism's objection of parochialness, so we draw a blank there. The objection is supported by stories of people to whom our styles seem mistaken or absurd, or of earlier styles of thought alien to ours now; and it is enough that the stories can be told, even if they are false, to make the point that other styles are possible. Whenever we extrapolate from the styles of some to the styles of all we risk flouting both fact and logic.

So what is it about *our* ways of respecting the constraints of reason, which we must share with others? Wisdom warned against paying too much respect to argument styles and the advice is worth attention. So is rationalism's advice that we should push back to basic reasons comprehensively shared as a precondition of engaging in discussion with others. Combining the two, we should push back to reasons without sticking unduly to our own institutionalized practices of argument. As Wisdom shows, to structure an argument deductively is to put it in a form occurring inessentially with respect to its conclusiveness since deductive forms are ultimately restructurable into arguments depending only on the comparison of cases. And this is a valuable point: there can be conclusive reasoning without our own institution of employing rules which guarantee the transmission of truth, so that there is no theoretical need to posit, or to hope for, universal acceptance of the principles of valid inference. In heeding rationalism's advice to push back to basics we do well not to stick with truths of logic, not only because they are an easy victim of relativism's objection, but also because there is a better answer to the question. In spite of the diversity of the ways in which we respect the constraints of reason, we ultimately heed them by our actions in respecting the constraints of the comparison of cases, either indirectly by honouring our institutional practices or directly by the discernment of parity and difference.

But what must we share of our ways with others? All along this has been a troublesome question because of relativism's pointer to an apparent absence of commensurability across times and cultures. There seems to be nothing we *have* to share with aliens, let us call them, except for a common restriction on action. They could not learn *our* ways of reasoning without a respect for the constraints of parity, since access to our scheme demands it, and we could not learn *their* ways since we cannot reason without it. If we do not share with aliens a common disposition to be constrained by similar and different cases we should lack not only the possibility of understanding them, but also the possibility of instructing them in our own ways of thought. The aliens lack access to us, just as we lack access to them, and the problem is to build a bridge for two-way traffic. If we set the price of engagement with others by our demands for a respect for parity, our demands must be theirs as well. And this shared practice gives a sense to the rationalist claim that in culturally distinct groups the final constraints on judgment are and must be of the same general nature irrespective of differences in outlook.

Unexpectedly this thought is supported by contingent evidence usually put to the service of relativism. An argument for saying that anthropologists and their native subjects cannot initially engage on the basis of a shared core of belief, either *a priori* or about the world, is simply that what the subjects mean must first be grasped. The anthropologist must start by learning how 'particulars of experience are ordered into clusters and patterns *specific to a culture*' and so 'learn which of the possible judgements of sameness are accepted by their society' as being relevant to the use of a term:

> When the anthropologist Bulmer visited the Karam of New Guinea he found that many of the instances of what we would call 'bird' were referred to as 'yakt'. He also found that instances of bats were included amongst the 'yakt', while instances of cassowaries were scrupulously denied admittance to the taxon. Objects were clustered in different ways, and the analogies that it is possible to discern amongst phenomena were channelled along different paths. Nevertheless, it was not too difficult to learn 'yakt': the task simply involved noting what the Karam pointed out as 'yakt' until it was possible to pick them out as well as the Karam did.[4]

The passage is intended to favour the relativist claim that there is no special core of belief which the learner must share with the natives. It actually shows something rather different: although there may be no shared beliefs about meanings, access to a society presupposes the ability to discern significant similarities and differences, from the subjects' behaviour, to see how they cluster objects into sorts. And this can occur only if the subjects, in picking out instances of yakts from instances of non-yakts, are restricted in their actions by their own perceptions of similarity and difference. The anthropologist could not learn which comparabilities speak for yakts unless the subjects pointed to arrays of instances comparable in the ways that do. However divergently the learner and the natives may carve up their experiences, they both must be constrained by parity in their ascriptive behaviour. Like us, the natives have a need for some restrictions on the scope of terms. And the restrictions *they* need are the same as the ones *we* need.

But does this matter? The answer is that it matters greatly if we are to make sense of aliens' ways. The relativist problem of engaging with 'other cultures' is just the problem of engaging with other people when neither we nor they comprehend each other's scheme of thought. Each initiate must learn from the ground up in the manner of the anthropologist Bulmer, or the child in Kuhn's example:

> Father points to a bird, saying 'Look Johnny, there's a swan'. A short time later Johnny himself points to a bird, saying, 'Daddy, another swan'. He has not yet, however, learned what swans are and must be corrected: 'No, Johnny, that's a goose'. Johnny's next identification of a swan proves to be correct, but his next 'goose' is, in fact, a duck, and he is again set straight. After a few more such encounters, however, each with its appropriate correction or reinforcement, Johnny's ability to identify these waterfowl is as great as his father's.[5]

In this 'mode of learning in its purest form' Kuhn says, 'the primary pedagogical tool is ostention'; and the learner 'has learned all this without acquiring, or at least without needing to acquire, even one criterion for identifying swans, geese or ducks'. He learns from the ground up by learning from exemplary instances and 'assimilating them is part of the socialization procedure by which Johnny is made part of that community and, in the process, learns about the world which the community inhabits'.[6]

Kuhn's case goes beyond the story about Bulmer although it describes the same mode of learning from parallel cases with its implication that a respect for parallels is shared as common ground. His discussion repositions the rationalist thesis of common ground by demonstrating the dispensability of general identifying criteria in the learning procedure which the relativist himself endorses. The 'rationalist *v.* relativist' confrontation is based on their common premise that such criteria must be found and, as Kuhn implies, the premise is not needed. It is no argument *for* relativism to point out that it is always possible to envisage circumstances in which the criteria or standards applied by one group of people are different from or inconsistent with those applied by another group, precisely because it is no defence *against* relativism to seek criteria which will pick out universally, across cultures, the one 'right' identifying reference of a predicate or description. The argument is reinforced by a story of Wisdom's linking Bulmer's and Kuhn's:

> A child asks, 'What is a greyhound?' His father replies, 'A greyhound is a dog of a certain sort'. 'I know', says the child, 'but what sort?' 'Well', his father says, 'A greyhound is a dog in which the power of weight ratio....' But his mother interrupts. 'Look', she says, 'That's a greyhound, and remember your uncle's dog, Entry Badge, well that was a greyhound. But now that' she says, pointing to a Borzoi, 'is not a greyhound, and even that' she says, pointing to a whippet, 'is not'. Or perhaps she recalls the rhyme:
>
> A foot like a cat, a tail like a rat,
> A back like a rake, a head like a snake,
>
> and so on. In short the mother replies with instances of what is and what is not a greyhound or by comparing greyhounds with what they are not, and these two procedures merge into one.[7]

The story points to the primary identity of rationalist and relativist aims. Rationalism wanted common ground which all must share in advance of engagement. Relativism argued that this is contrary-to-fact; at each encounter one has to learn case-by-case from scratch and there is likely to be a new lesson each time. Both views make the mistake of supposing that their aims are incompatible, instead of just being different. The distance between the views is just that difference of style in Wisdom's story between teaching by reference to something true of instances in general, and teaching what is true of them instance after instance; or between the demand for a principle in virtue of which an instance is true, and the presentation of instances in virtue of which the principle is true. The relativist's procedure implies what the rationalist wants, since a person cannot learn from another person case-by-case unless they share a form of action jointly constrained by differences and parallels between the cases in question. Although ways of settling issues about what is so vary contingently with different outlooks, cultures and backgrounds, if we share with others a respect for the constraints of comparable cases we share enough to have a common form of action in learning and teaching, and a bridgehead for objective engagement through discussion.

Yet this foothold for objectivity begs a central question. Can people sharing the forms of life distinctive of a culture be judged by any standards other than their own? Relativism answers 'no'; there is no extramural standpoint for judging intramural differences, and no single standard capable of adjudicating between conflicts across systems.

This relativist argument – that a plurality of systems prevents any assessments across them – seems mistaken, if only because we often do judge other cultures on particular issues. We may value the virtues of our system of science over the deficiencies of other systems giving an impoverished grasp of physical nature, and argue convincingly that physics has at least greatly advanced our understanding of the material world, and that this is a presumption in its favour which cannot be ignored.[8] Admittedly the argument is harder to sustain against refusals to value the results of theory and technology, and it may rest more securely on the ubiquitous desire for self-protection and the satisfaction of people's needs in the face of nature.[9] Armed with this thought, in particular cases there are compelling reasons for asserting the superiority of our ways. If we range the capabilities of Tudor medicine against the natural forces it engaged, and set this beside our capabilities now, the distance between them is not only one of measurable fact but also one in which the facts count decisively towards our view. And this is so if we contrast our own views' control over nature with that of the rationale of Paracelsus, or of beliefs in witchcraft. The pull away from relativism is strongest with the thought that we share with people of alien cultures a common physiology and a common interface with nature, and that the natural obstacles to the survival and success of other people are similar to those we ourselves must deal with. It is a short step to the conclusion that a scheme of things which deals badly with people by dealing badly with nature, like Tudor medicine, is not to be preferred to a scheme of things which does better. Since all men face the world as physical beings despite their heterogeneous perceptions of it, we may often bring the beliefs of others within the orbit of assessment without special pleading.

Yet judgments of this kind are limited to particular aspects of a culture broadly characterized by the feature that minimal penetration of the cultural fabric in question is needed prior to judgment. There is no necessity to understand the wider forms of life in which the criticized practices are embedded. The claim to superiority of our physics or medicine, for example, is tested in confrontations with nature and not in debates with the aliens, and beyond the assumption that nature – including the physical side of humans – is uniform the standard is one of practical results. If relativism's premise that plurality rules out judgments about other systems is overstated, it is a warning that although the ranking of achievements in *this* way is possible, it is no answer to the problem of comprehending, let alone assessing, alien schemes of thought.

One way of identifying different systems is to separate them by the test of whether an array of beliefs essential to one of them is held to be false in the other, encouraging the idea that the difference that matters between aliens and ourselves is the conflict between our respective truth-values. Yet the idea that truth-value conflicts are definitive of cultural differences is ultimately unsatisfactory. Access to a system of thought radically different from one's own requires more than the knowledge that it fails to respect the truth-values one's own culture assigns. A person must also understand how aliens' ways of thinking bear on the truth-values they assign. Hence the importance of Wittgenstein's point that the price of access is often a shift in one's own view of the world bringing a person to 'look at the world in a different way'. As he describes them, such shifts can be 'conversions of a special kind'.

An aspect of conceptual conversions emphasized by Kuhn is that other perspectives cannot, or can no longer be, perceived as being genuine alternatives. They are 'a dead option' to use James's expression, and as James says, 'No tendency to act on it exists in us to any degree'; it does not appeal 'as a real possibility to him to whom it is proposed' or appear as a rival or a competitor to the view which a person has made his own.[10] 'Dead options' may be taken to be false, obsolete or incoherent, or just be ignored; but their special feature lies in the impossibility of a person's seriously taking them to be true, or possibly true, without disrupting the framework of his own scheme of belief. The choice is one between something that is within the limits of one's understanding and which might be acted on, and something that is not. From our point of view, for example, beliefs in magic or the efficacy of oracles are as a matter of fact false and could not possibly be, or have been, true at any time; as Wittgenstein might say, our system 'forbids us to believe it'; there is no place prepared for them in our picture of the world. And here consistency prevails; the alien picture can be seen on the whole to be credible only if our own picture ceases to function over much of its range.

One consequence of forgetting this feature is a tendency to judge relativism by its failure to give a satisfying answer to a question which is unanswerable in the context in which it is asked. The question 'Which of these belief systems is, on the whole and all things considered, closer to the truth?' is fine in a situation where the systems compared can be seen as options 'among the mind's possibilities', as James says. The gap between them is narrow enough for conversion to be superfluous, and with a narrow gap there is no excuse for relativism: we may look on different pictures as being, potentially, the same picture or at least as being rivals. The excuse of relativism lies in the fact that we cannot always do this since *some* pictures of the world are for us non-starters in any competitive stakes. They are ruled out as proper topics of the question because the idea of their being genuine possibilities is too remote from our grasp. Dead options, James remarks, go against 'all such factors of belief as fear and hope, prejudice and passion, imitation and partisanship, the circumpressure of our caste and set'.[11] An enlightened relativism refuses to rise to the bait by trying to answer the question, and it is right to refuse. What the relativist should seek is an understanding of an adequate model for change, one not governed by the idea that change is synonymous with the replacement of false beliefs by true ones, but by the idea of a dialogue between 'fields of view' maintaining their objectivity through a mutual responsiveness to criticism.[12]

NOTES

Chapter 1   The human contribution: William James and Thomas Kuhn

1 Thomas Kuhn, *The Structure of Scientific Revolutions*, Chicago, 1970, p. 186; *The Essential Tension*, p. 321 and note referring to criticism by Lakatos, Shapere and Scheffler; Hugo Meynell, 'Science, the Truth and Thomas Kuhn', *Mind*, January 1975, p. 87; Roger Trigg, *Reason and Commitment*, pp. 99-119; see generally I. Scheffler, *Science and Subjectivity*, Indianapolis, 1967, chapter 1.

2 Kuhn, SSR, pp. 94, 199-200; ET, pp. 329-31; *Criticism and the Growth of Knowledge*, eds Lakatos and Musgrave, Cambridge, 1970, p. 262.

3 William James, 'The Will to Believe', Collected Papers, Harvard, 1979.

4 James, *Pragmatism and Four Essays on the Meaning of Truth*, New American Library, 1974; ed. Ralph Barton Perry, lecture two, esp. pp. 50-1, p. 142.

5 ibid., p. 142.

6 Richard Rorty, *Consequences of Pragmatism*, The Harvester Press, 1982, p. 165; for a brief modern look at James see Morton White's chapter 8 in *Science and Sentiment in America*, Oxford, 1972, esp. 'The Other James' pp. 204-16.

7 James, *Letters*.

8 James, *Pragmatism*, p. 28.

9 James, *Letters*; in 1907 he writes optimistically to Henry James,

> I have just finished the proofs of a little book called 'Pragmatism' which even you *may* enjoy reading. It is a very 'sincere' and, from the point of view of ordinary philosophy – professorial manners, a very unconventional utterance, not particularly original at any one point, yet, in the midst of the literature of that way of thinking, which it represents, with just that amount of squeak or shrillness in the voice that enables one book to *tell*, when others don't, to supersede its brethren, and be treated later as 'representative'. I shouldn't be surprised if ten years hence it should be rated as 'epochmaking', for of the definitive triumph of that general way of thinking I can entertain no doubt whatever – I believe it to be something quite like the Protestant reformation.

The Letters of William James, Longman, 1926, vol. II, p. 279.

10 James, *Pragmatism*, p. 20.

11 Kuhn, ET, chapter 12; see footnote p. 302, and pp. 307–8.

12 C. S. Peirce, especially 'The Fixation of Belief', 1877; 'How to Make Our Ideas Clear', 1878.

13 James, *Pragmatism*, p. 165.

Chapter 2 *The two faces of objectivity*

1 See J. Austin, 'Truth'; P. F. Strawson, 'Truth', in Pitcher (ed.), *Truth*, Prentice Hall, 1964.

2 The transformation has become unselfconsciously standard. F. N. Sibley puts the argument in aesthetics,

> Where there are disagreements, we can bring forward procedures, an apparatus of proof, to settle whether something really is red or only seems so. But aesthetic terms, it may be insisted, are quite otherwise and no considerations bear on whether they have been correctly predicated of something or not. They deal with subjective, not objective matters.

Sibley adds, 'Such an extreme conclusion I suspect again is hasty', 'Philosophy and the Arts', *Inaugural Lectures*, 1965–7, Lancaster, 1967, p. 145. John Passmore, in the case of history:

If the test of objectivity is that there are regular ways of settling issues, by the use of which men of whatever party can be brought to see what actually happened, then I do not see how one can doubt the objectivity of history ... 'The Objectivity of History', *Philosophy*, April 1958, p. 109.

Quine says, scientific theories on all sorts of useful and useless topics are sustained by empirical controls, partial and devious though they be.
It is bitter irony that so vital a matter as the difference between good and evil should have no comparable claim to objectivity. No wonder there have been efforts since earliest times to work a justification of moral values into the fabric of what might pass for factual science.

'On the Nature of Moral Values', p. 43, in Goldman and Kim (eds), *Value and Morals*, 1978.

3 There is a touch of this in James, and *Pragmatism* was dedicated to Mill 'whom my fancy likes to picture as our leader were he alive today'.

4 C. S. Stevenson, *Ethics and Language*, New Haven, 1944, pp. 237, 209.

5 For a concise statement of the idea see Scheffler, *Science and Subjectivity*, chapter 1.

6 Richard Rorty, *Philosophy and the Mirror of Nature*, Blackwell, 1980, pp. 338-9.

7 Thomas Nagel, *Moral Questions*, Cambridge, 1979, chapter 14; Sir Karl Popper, *Objective Knowledge*, Oxford, 1974, chapter 3.

8 See Renford Bambrough, 'Universals and Family Resemblances', *PAS* 1961, p. 217.

9 James, *Pragmatism*, p. 168.

Chapter 3   A role for observation

1 Karl Popper, *The Logic of Scientific Discovery*, Hutchinson, 1972, chapter 1.

2 The best example is Pollock, *Knowledge and Justification*, Princeton,

1974; see N. Rescher, *The Coherence Theory of Truth*, Oxford, 1973, for the assignment of 'presumptive' truth prior to consistency screening, pp. 53–9.

3 A. J. Ayer, *The Central Questions of Philosophy*, Penguin, 1978.

4 W. V. O. Quine, 'Epistemology Naturalized', in *Ontological Relativity and Other Essays*, New York, 1969, p. 75.

5 'What is to count as observation now can be settled in terms of the stimulation of sensory receptors, let consciousness fall where it may', Quine, op. cit., p. 84; see pp. 82–4, and 'Grades of Theoreticity' in Foster and Swanson (eds.), *Experience and Theory*, Amherst, 1970, pp. 2–8; *The Web of Belief*, with J. S. Ullian, Random House, 1970, chapter 2; 'The Nature of Natural Knowledge, in S. Guttenplan (ed.) *Mind and Language*, Oxford, 1975, pp. 72–3.

6 See Richard Schuldenfrei, 'Quine in Perspective', *The Journal of Philosophy*, January 1972; and Harold Morick, 'Observation and Subjectivity in Quine', *Canadian Journal of Philosophy*, 1974.

7 Quine, 'Grades of Theoreticity', pp. 2–3.

8 Quine, *The Web of Belief*, p. 16; 'Epistemology Naturalized', p. 89; see *Word and Object*, MIT, 1960, p. 44.

9 See Sandra Harding, 'Making Sense of Observation Sentences', *Ratio*, 1975.

10 Otto Neurath, 'Protocol Sentences', in A. J. Ayer (ed.), *Logical Positivism*, Glencoe, 1959, p. 201.

11 Quine, 'Epistemology Naturalized', p. 89.

12 Quine, 'Grades of Theoreticity', p. 2.

13 Neurath, op. cit., p. 202.

14 Quine, *Word and Object*, pp. 11–12.

15 Peirce, Letter to Lady Welby, in P. Weiner, *Peirce, Selected Writings*, Dover, 1958, p. 398.

16 Kuhn, SSR, pp. 170–1.

17 James, *Pragmatism*, p. 50.

18 ibid. p. 51.

19 James, 'Humanism and Truth', in Ralph Barton Perry (ed.), *Pragmatism and Four Essays on the Meaning of Truth*, pp. 248–9.

20 James, *Pragmatism*, p. 59.

21 ibid., p. 161.

22 ibid., p. 53.

23 ibid., p. 140.

24 James, *Humanism and Truth*, pp. 254-5, 250.

25 ibid., p. 250.

Chapter 4   Certainty and human action: Wittgenstein

1 Wittgenstein, *On Certainty*, Blackwell, Oxford, 1969, 94, 105; see also 102, 144, 410.

2 ibid., 136, 341, 655.

3 ibid., 234.

4 ibid., 337.

5 ibid., 151, 342.

6 ibid., 125.

7 ibid., 88.

8 ibid., 204, 110; for discussion of some of the points raised here see R. A. Shiner, 'Wittgenstein and the Foundations of Knowledge', *PAS* January 1978.

9 Wittgenstein, *On Certainty*, 144, 142, 140, 225.

10 Wittgenstein, *Remarks on Colour*, Blackwell, 1978, 348; *OC*, 234.

11 Wittgenstein, *On Certainty*, 102.

12 ibid., 614, 155, 419, 279.

13 D. Z. Phillips, 'Wittgenstein's Full Stop', in I. Block (ed.), *Perspectives in the Philosophy of Wittgenstein* Blackwell, 1981, p. 191. Phillips has religious or ritualistic responses in mind but the idea applies quite generally to the response of sticking with certainty. Phillips rightly insists that 'the response need not be related to that which surrounds it as a hypothesis is related to the evidence for it, a conclusion is related to its premises, or a belief to its reasons'.

14 ibid., 613.

15 ibid., 378, 219.

16 ibid., 256.

17 ibid., 96-7, 616-17.

18 ibid., 291.

19 Hume, *Enquiries Concerning The Human Understanding*, sec. v., pt. 2. The passage fascinated James well before his mature thinking about pragmatism, see *Principles of Psychology*, vol. II, Henry Holt, New York, 1931, p. 295.

20 Quine, *Word and Object*, p. 44.

21 Wittgenstein, *On Certainty*, 521, 504, 243, 414, 550-1; see 178, 308, 484; and *Remarks on Colour*, 350.

22 Wittgenstein, *On Certainty*, 674, 662.

23 James, *Pragmatism*, p. 145.

Chapter 5   Reason and particular cases: John Wisdom

1 For discussions of Wisdom's argument see Dilman, *Induction and Deduction*, Blackwell, 1973, pp. 115-20; and Bambrough, *Moral Scepticism and Moral Knowledge*, Routledge & Kegan Paul, 1979, chapter 8. Much of Wisdom's best work on this topic remains in his unpublished but widely circulated lectures on 'Proof and Explanation'. For a glimpse of them see Yalden-Thomson, 'The Virginia Lectures' in J. R. Bambrough (ed.), *Wisdom: 12 Essays*, Blackwell, 1974.

2 Susan Haack, 'The Justification of Deduction', *Mind*, January 1976; see also Barnes and Bloor, 'Relativism, Rationalism and the Sociology of Knowledge', in M. Hollis and S. Lukes (eds.), *Rationality and Relativism*, Cambridge, 1982, pp. 40-3.

3 J. S. Mill, *A System of Logic*, Longman, 1952, book II, chapter I, sec. 3.

4 Haack, op. cit., p. 118.

5 Wisdom, *Paradox and Discovery*, Blackwell, 1965, p. 6.

6 ibid., p. 6.

7 See Lewis Carroll, 'What the Tortoise said to Achilles', *Mind*, 4, 1895.

8 Wisdom, op. cit., p. 145.

Chapter 6   *Rationality, relativism and objectiveness*

1 Wittgenstein, *On Certainty*, 609, 612.

2 ibid., 262, 92, 209, 206, 233.

3 M. Hollis, 'The Social Destruction of Reality', in *Rationality and Relativism*, p. 84.

4 Barnes and Bloor, 'Relativism, Rationalism and the Sociology of Knowledge', in M. Hollis and S. Lukes (eds), *Rationality and Relativism*, pp. 37–8.

5 Kuhn, ET, p. 309.

6 ibid., pp. 312–13.

7 Wisdom, *Paradox and Discovery*, pp. 69–70.

8 See Charles Taylor, 'Rationality', in *Rationality and Relativism*, p. 102.

9 James noted the danger of 'the practical control of nature newly put into our hands by scientific ways of thinking'; 'One may even fear that the *being* of man may be crushed by his own powers.... He may drown like a child in a bath-tub, who has turned on the water and who cannot turn it off.' *Pragmatism*, p. 123.

10 James, 'The Will to Believe', sec. I, II.

11 ibid., sec. III.

12 The idea is latent in James. See 'Humanism and Truth', pp. 249–50; and Rorty, *Philosophy and the Mirror of Nature*, part 3; *Consequences of Pragmatism*, chapter 9.

Index